跟雅思考官
Simon
学听力 2.0

王辰雨　主编

北京理工大学出版社
BEIJING INSTITUTE OF TECHNOLOGY PRESS

图书在版编目（CIP）数据

跟雅思考官 Simon 学听力 2.0 / 王辰雨主编 . -- 北京：
北京理工大学出版社 , 2022.9
ISBN 978-7-5763-1667-4

Ⅰ . ①跟… Ⅱ . ①王… Ⅲ . ① IELTS －听说教学－自
学参考资料 Ⅳ . ① H319.9

中国版本图书馆 CIP 数据核字 (2022) 第 160391 号

出版发行 / 北京理工大学出版社有限责任公司
社　　　址 / 北京市海淀区中关村南大街 5 号
邮　　　编 / 100081
电　　　话 / （010）68914775（总编室）
　　　　　　（010）82562903（教材售后服务热线）
　　　　　　（010）68944723（其他图书服务热线）
印　　　刷 / 三河市京兰印务有限公司
开　　　本 / 889 毫米 ×1194 毫米　1/16
印　　　张 / 8.25
字　　　数 / 200 千字
版　　　次 / 2022 年 9 月第 1 版　2022 年 9 月第 1 次印刷
定　　　价 / 79.00 元

责任编辑 / 时京京
文案编辑 / 时京京
责任校对 / 刘亚男
责任印制 / 李志强

图书出现印装质量问题，请拨打售后服务热线，本社负责调换

目录
contents

雅思听力对大部分本科四六级通过的学生来说，裸考一般能到5.5~5分，包括其中的填空题和选择题的题型，大家也都非常熟悉。理论上来说，听力不需要太多的方法论，因为未经培训的母语人士也可以获得一个不错的听力分数。但从笔者多年的实际教学经验来看，考生们普遍对这种语速较快、有特定使用场景的对话/独白还不够熟悉，对预判答案、拼写、同义替换、抓取信号词等环节不够熟练。

下面是Simon老师关于听力考试四个部分的基本技巧介绍，大家可以看一下。

Key technique!

Use the breaks to read ahead

- **before** each section starts
- in the **middle** of each section
  (except in section 4)
- at the **end** of each section

本书针对雅思两大题型：填空题和选择题分别进行了讲解，同时配有难度梯度的练习题。除了方法之外，听力需要大量的练习，这一点毋庸置疑。鸭圈还有一本听力词汇书叫《鸭圈雅思真题词2.0》比较适合做听写练习，主要针对过去8年雅思听力Part1和Part4做听写练习。如果要刷题的话可以使用《雅思听力真题还原2.0》，无论是题型还是套卷练习都比较适合考前自测。同时，一定要养成总结错题的习惯，所有的错题都要进行归纳和整理。可以像这样做一个表格：

题型:	错题来源:
□ 选择题 □ 总结/填空题 □ 判断题 □ 信息配对题 □ 段落大意题 □ 其他题型	题干: 阅读原文:
错因归类: □ 单词不认识 □ 听力/原文不理解 □ 题干读不懂 □ 信号词没找到 □ 同替没找对/识别 □ 其他原因	 正确答案&解析:

（该表格来自《雅思效率笔记本》）

及时对自己的错因进行归纳，学生**需要刷题的数量，更需要质量**。

本书从考生的几大弊病出发，侧重于方法的讲授，同学们先通过《鸭圈雅思真题词2.0》积累词汇，再通过《跟雅思考官Simon学听力2.0》学习方法，最后用《雅思听力真题还原2.0》刷题，这也是鸭圈雅思陪考营过去三年学生的学习方法，十分有效。最后，笔者能力有限，本书不足之处，还请读者通过"鸭圈留学考试"公众号与学生交流。

鸭圈雅思教研组 王辰雨
2022.8

填空题方法论

听写 / 拼写

单词拼写错误是学生在听力和写作考试中都会犯的错误，如果你总是拼不对单词，以下是笔者的建议：

1 使用Word文档来写作，它会告诉你哪些单词拼错了；

2 如果你用手写，记得手里下载一个查单词的APP，随时检查，比如Merriam-Webster Dictionary；

3 做一个单词本，每错一个单词，就把错词抄到本子上，或者使用鸭圈的《雅思效率笔记本》，像这样：

错词	正确的单词
grag, garaj	garage
clasical	calssical
planed	planned
city councel	city council
combinaiton	combination
atitude, attitud	attitude
controle	control

把容易错的单词写在便签纸上，贴在电脑、书桌、甚至墙上。

4 单词本上的错词要不定期做拼写测试；

5 有些同学可能会去记一些所谓的拼写规律，比如词根词缀，但从实际效果来说，直接记单词可能更省事。

当学生觉得自己背完了，应该如何检测拼写呢？学生可以随机从《雅思听力真题还原2.0》中选取一套题的答案，然后照着读出来（如果你发现你读都读不出的话，那肯定拼不出了）并录音。接着听录音，做听写练习，看看自己是否能写对。

接下来学生一起做几道单词拼写练习。

1 .... 2 .... 3 .... 4 ....
5 .... 6 .... 7 .... 8 ....
9 .... 10 ....

1. refreshments 2. plates 3. laboratory 4. reliable 5. pattern 6. attitude 7. factories
8. creature 9. priorities 10. images

1 .... 2 .... 3 .... 4 ....
5 .... 6 .... 7 .... 8 ....
9 .... 10 ....

1. hostel 2. cycling 3. curtains 4. attitude 5. software 6. patients (你听出"s"了吗？)
7. comfortable 8. analysis 9. secondary 10. cattle

1 .... 2 .... 3 .... 4 ....
5 .... 6 .... 7 .... 8 ....

1. budget 2. damage 3. resources 4. unnecessary 5. scientist 6. superiority 7. absence
8. temporary 9. fountain 10. culture

大写、复数、字数

考生们经常问笔者："打头字母是否可以大写，比如答案是Central Station写成central station"；"如果正确答案是复数但笔者没有加s会不会扣分"。

笔者的答案是：在雅思考试中，任何字母的大写或不大写都是可以接受的，都算正确；如果题目有语法考察的情况下，如"The journey take three **hour**"这时肯定算错（实际考试中这样的情况最多），而如果答案单复数都不影响题目的话，算对。

考生们有时很难确定填空题的单复数，特别是当他们没有听出是否有"s"时，所以是否要加s需要取决于语法。咱们来看《剑桥雅思真题13》里的两题：

1 includes recipes to strengthen your **bones**

2 Catarina Miranda focused on the behaviour of urban and rural blackbirds.

第一题的bones是对的，这个空不能填单数，因为这里如果你用单数的话，读者会想到底是哪一块骨头呢？这句话的本意应该是指所有的骨头；第二题用behaviour和behaviours都是可以的，单数表示一个整体的行为，而复数代表由一个个动作组成的集合。

咱们来看下面这几个填空，看你能否写对：

1 Bring two forms of .... (identification/identifications).

2 You may use your own .... (pen/pens) in the exam.

3 Please park between the .... (line/lines).

4 Entry is only permitted to registered .... (student/students).

5 The lecturer will leave plenty of .... (time/times) for questions.

答案：

1 identification 单数　2 pen和pens都可以　3 lines 复数　4 students 复数　5 time 单数

在听力考试填空题的题目要求通常有如下几种：

1 "Write **ONE WORD ONLY** for each answer"；这个要求很简单，只能写一个单词，如果你写"a pen"就是错的。

2 "Write **ONE WORD AND/OR A NUMBER** for each answer"；这个要求意味着你的答案可以是一个单词，也可以是一个数字，抑或是一个单词加一个数字，比如"12th September"。

3 "Write **NO MORE THAN TWO WORDS AND/OR A NUMBER** for each answer"；理论上来说答案可以是一个单词；一个数字；一个单词和一个数字；两个单词；两个单词和一个数字，比如15 Bank Road。不过从实战角度来说，答案通常都会是两个单词或两个单词加数字。

4 "Write **NO MORE THAN THREE WORDS** for each answer"；碰到这个要求通常都需要写三个单词（理论上是一至三个单词都行）。

请注意： 连词会被算作是一个单词，比如hard-working；通常答案都不会包含缩写，如doesn't。

画关键词

画关键词在阅读考试中非常重要，听力也是。学生要利用对白间隙的时间去画题干中的关键词。比如下面两道题的，这会画出哪几个关键词呢？

1 According to the schedule, the meeting will take place at ....
2 The decision will mean that full-time employees are allowed to ....for free.

同一个题干不需要画太多，以上是笔者画出的关键词，画词并没有标准答案，仅供参考。

通常情况下，当你听到一个关键词时，答案都在它后面。但有时候，也会出现答案会在关键词之前的情况，就比如下面这道题：

Undiscovered material may be damaged by ....（《剑桥雅思真题7》）

这道题通常学生会画出undiscovered material和damaged by，同时预判答案会出现在关键词之后。学生来看一下原文：

Don't make fires, however romantic it may seem. It's really dangerous in dry areas, and you can easily burn priceless undiscovered material by doing so.

这里的burn by和题干的damaged by是同义词，而doing so指代的是之前的make fires，所以正确答案是**fires**。

陷阱题

听力中有很多陷阱，对白中会出现很多疑似答案，或是给出一个答案之后很快又"变卦"。咱们一起来做一道《剑桥雅思真题5》中的题：

1 Cost to join per year (without current student card): £ ....

2 Number of items allowed (members of public): ....

3 Creative Writing class: Held on .... evenings

第一题：

Does it cost anything to join? Well, its free for students here, but otherwise its 125 pounds per year or 25 pounds if you have got a current student card from another college.

当学生看到**£**时就应该知道，后面肯定需要填一个金额，所以听的时候要特别留心数字。这里的otherwise指代的其实是题干中的without current student card。

第二题：

We allowed 12 items borrow at any one times if you are student that including DVD, CD and videos. However, its only 8 items from member of the public.

当学生看到题干中的Number of items时，知道空格处需要填一个数字。在通常情况下，听力原文中However后面的内容才是考点。通过members of public这个信号词，不难得出答案。

第三题：

A：Is other classes in Library? yes He is here on Thursday evening.

B：Oh no, sorry Friday. He just changed it. you can contact him by email in library.

根据题干，有经验的同学就能够判断出来空格中应该是填某个星期，稍加留意就会发现原文中先说了Thursday，然后很快改为Friday。

地图题是有顺序的

有时候学生会碰到地图题，它其实是填空题的一种，下面这幅图来自《剑桥雅思真题7》。

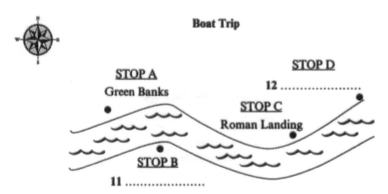

很多学生惧怕听力地图题因为她们非常容易"找不着北"，不知道应该看哪。这里笔者给大家介绍一个小技巧：永远盯着第一个题目。地图题的答案出现是有顺序的，所以学生要盯着第一题的内容。比如上面这幅图，学生的耳朵要留心11题的"**STOP B**"，然后顺着题号留心"**STOP D**"。

听力 part4

听力考试中最难的部分就是part4了，因为它持续10分钟，中间没有任何停顿；你只能听到独白，通常是一大段演讲；讲述者的语速通常较快（相对于part2/3来说）；词汇的难度较大（相对于part1来说）且有很多同义词替换，还会出现一些学术词汇。

笔者通常会跟同学们说，不要太过于担心Part4，而要把注意力放到Part1~3上。这听起来似乎是一个不太像建议的建议，但却非常实用——抓住自己可以抓住的，听懂自己可以听懂的，做对自己可以做对的。下面是笔者对这四个部分的得分建议：

Part1：做对10道题

Part2：做对8道题

Part3：做对7道题

Part4：做对5道题

你可以大概算一下，按照上面的正确率，你可以拿到雅思听力7分，而你的part4其实只需要对5道题即可。当然，如果你有更高分数的要求，那么就要适当提高Part3和Part4的正确率了。同时，笔者告诉大家一个练习Part4的好方法：

1 从《剑桥雅思真题系列》或《雅思听力真题还原2.0》中挑一个Part4出来；

2 把正确答案直接填回到空格中；

3 填完以后放录音，跟着录音边停边看，搞懂答案为什么正确；如有必要，可重复听几次；

4 把听力文稿中的同义词组和题干中的关键词都画出来，列成同替词表。坚持这么做，你会发现Part4也会变得越来越简单。

填空题练习

If a child turns two but is still **1** .... ,
parents start to worry.

Parents often **2**..................... this problem, hoping that their child will soon
3..................... ....

One reason for late language development could be a delay in the child's **4**.................... ....

Delayed language development could also be caused by **5**.................... or .... problems.

 第2题

These are the 10 most liveable cities in the world, according to monocle.com

1 top- .... education and welfare

2 integration for immigrants to increase its ....

3 greatly .... public transportation

4 innovative, mixed-use .... incorporating cycling paths

5 hidden under the .... of a neon-lit mega city

6 a small-town ....

7 world-class shopping and business ....

8 Australia's cultural ....

9 a big push to .... traffic congestion

10 integration between city life and the ....

第3题

1 Eastman started manufacturing celluloid film in ....

2 The "Kodak" was available to consumers from the year ....

3 It was bought by normal people because it was .... and ....

4 The camera was able to take .... pictures before a new film was needed.

 第4题

Fill the gaps below using a maximum of three words and/or numbers.

1 The minimum notice period to arrange a visit is ....

2 You may send your booking form by post, fax or ....

3 If there are no places for your first choice, you will be offered an ....

4 On arrival, you should go to the .... between 9 and 9.15.

5 The maximum number of guests is ....

 第5题

Fill the gaps below with a MAXIMUM of THREE WORDS.

Common mistakes when writing a CV:

1 Having a .... CV without a good structure.

2 Writing .... , with long paragraphs or sentences, will lose people's ....

3 It's often hard to spot your own ....

4 Unexplained gaps in the dates on your CV will raise questions about what you might be ....

5 A gap in the dates could cause an employer to think ....

that doesn't just mean another city

Amsterdam is one of the places that is becoming increasingly popular as a destination for a sort of "1.............................. ....". Amsterdam University College offers courses in English in order to attract 2..................... from all over the world. The amount of British students has 3..................... over the last year, and they expect the numbers to increase considerably when tuition 4..................... in the UK rise next year.

Community service is the practice of 1..................... or 2..................... unpaid work. Examples of projects include cleaning a park, collecting items for 3..................... or cleaning 4..................... verges. Other examples include 5..................... children with learning disabilities or 6..................... money for the local area. Some students must do community service in order to receive their 7..................... .... "Service learning" means that students have to show how their work has 8..................... to their education.

Fill each gap with a maximum of three words.

The libraries of the future are still about equitable .... for our communities and our customers. However, what we do know is that we now have a 10% .... from traditional print material into the electronic world. So we've got to move to more digital faster.

But that requires a balance: we're not throwing out the print, but we need to .... to work within this .... It's a really exciting time to be a librarian, as we adapt to this changing way our customers are using information.

第9题

1 Over the last decade smokers across the country have been .... the defensive.

2 New York City is now taking the war against tobacco a .... with a new law that .... effect tomorrow, banning smoking outdoors.

3 The law aims to .... , if not eliminate, exposure to .... - .... smoke.

4 Officials also hope to discourage a new generation from .... the habit, sending out the message that it is no longer acceptable to .... in family-friendly places.

第10题

Fill each gap in the summaries below with ONE word.

1 She works in the .... field, and she has always wanted to offer her .... abroad.

2 He wanted to do something .... , and not just be a ....

3 She says that she's in a safe .... with friendly ....

4 She talks about the importance of grasping the .... of the people.

5 She thinks it's an amazing ....

6 He says it's about more than just reading a .... book or visiting the tourist ....

第11题

Beginning in the 1990s, the most 1..................... .... given for attending college had changed from reasons such as becoming an 2..................... in a field or helping others to the 3..................... .... a

lot of money. At the same time, compact disc players, 4..................... .... , personal computers, and cellular telephones all began to integrate into 5..................... ....
Madeline Levine criticised what she saw as a large change in American culture — "a shift away from 6..................... .... , spirituality, and integrity, and toward competition, materialism and disconnection."

 第12题

that would have seemed like science fiction

Aristotle called happiness the 1..................... .... , the end towards which all other things aim. The reason we want a big house, a nice car or a good job isn't that these things are intrinsically 2..................... , it's that we expect them to bring us happiness. The paradox of happiness is that even though the 3..................... conditions in our lives have improved 4..................... , we haven't actually gotten any happier. In the last few years there's been an 5..................... in research on happiness; we've learnt how things like income, education, 6..................... and 7..................... relate to it.

 第13题

Over the 1..................... of the last weekend, the local authority collected 20 tonnes of rubbish from one beach. It costs the authority a great 2..................... of money to collect the rubbish, but they take 3..................... in their beach, and they want to 4..................... visitors. The leader of the local council would like people to take 5..................... for their rubbish and take it home.

He believes that there is an 6..................... of personal responsibility, but that suppliers should also think about how they 7..................... their goods. He says that the council needs to attack the problem at both 8..................... .

第14题

John Dewey was America's 1..................... philosopher and philosopher of education. His ideas are important to education today because he recognised that each individual brings a certain 2..................... and 3..................... to his or her learning. He also understood the importance of learning in a group or 4..................... , learning from others that are 5..................... you. The essence of a democracy is that you have different 6..................... and you learn from each of them, and Dewey celebrated that. He would probably be 7..................... of the current system of education because it ignores the teaching 8..................... and what each student brings to the classroom.

第15题

It turns out that more than 10% of people, or about 10%, are left-handed. If both parents are right-handed, there's about a 2% chance your child is going to be a 1..................... . If one parent is left-handed, it's about 17%, and if both parents are lefties, there's about a 50% chance your child is also going to be left-handed, with guys 2..................... twice as often left-handed as girls.

So how do you tell what your child is going to be? (Well) when your baby is about six months of age, he or she may 3..................... to reach with their right hand, but very quickly will bring out their left hand, and it's not until a baby or a 4..................... is two years of age that we can really determine hand preference.

第16题

The fact is, multitasking is a 1..................... . Our brains can't do it. You simply become less efficient and more distracted, your error rate goes up 50 per cent, and it takes you twice as long to do the same task. Listen what Tim Jenkins has to say. He's the co- 2..................... of Point B, a leading business consulting firm.

Well I think there's a 3..................... out there, that folks that can multitask are more effective. There are times when it's just important to focus on one thing. I think we also need to give people permission to check out, to check out of the communications 4..................... temporarily to get things done; because when you're always on, when you're always online, you're always distracted, right, and the brain really is telling us that that is a very unproductive 5..................... to be in. So the always online organisation is actually the always unproductive organisation.

 第17题

The first thing any regular train user should do is to book their tickets in advance, 1..................... exactly 12 weeks in advance. Those ￡300 tickets to Manchester, you can get them for just ￡25 return if you go online. You go to a website called thetrainline.com, you fill in their ticket 2..................... system, and you'll get an email telling you when those tickets are available. Because they often 3..................... .... very quickly, so when you get that email, act straight away.

But, and I know this sounds a bit sneaky, don't actually buy them on thetrainline.com, because you'll have to pay a ￡1.50 booking fee, and if you're using your credit card another ￡1.50. Instead, 4..................... over to the East Coast website - you'd think that's only trains down the East coast from London up to Edinburgh - it's not; they will sell tickets for any trains anywhere in the UK, and they don't charge a booking fee, and they don't charge for credit card. So that's another two or three 5..................... saved.

If you haven't been able to buy a ticket a long 6..................... in advance, it is still worth remembering that up until 6 o'clock on the night before, you can still get Advance tickets. They won't be as cheap as the Super-Advance ones, 12 weeks in advance, but it's still 7..................... trying to buy them the night before.

There are six fundamental things that a city needs to get 1..................... . The first is order. Order means balance, 2..................... and repetition. But too much regularity can be soul- destroying; too much order feels rigid and 3..................... . It can be bleak, relentless and 4..................... . The ideal we're 5..................... is variety and order.

1 We spend about 10 hours a day sitting, which is an unprecedented .... activity.

2 There are significant health risks .... sitting, for instance decreased life ....

3 Diabetes, obesity, heart disease and cancer are things that you wouldn't intuitively associate with a sedentary ....

4 Our bodies .... lack of movement as a ....

1 In today's society we rely on .... and .... to access information.

2 We have to trust that a passport or driver's license has not been .... with.

3 Fingerprint, facial, iris and .... patterns are sources of biometric data.

4 We're identifying people at .... with facial recognition software.

5 As the technology .... , our identities will be better ....

 第21题

Quick exercise: Fill the gaps in the sentences below.

1 The first problem is that micro-plastics act like a .... , attracting other .... in the water, such as pesticides and .... retardants.

2 The second problem is that micro-plastics are complex polymers that the body cannot fully .... down.

3 Scientists have shown that the smallest particles, nano-plastics, can .... tissue membranes into fish cells. This could damage fish reproduction, ... and survival skills.

 第22题

In 1950, the world's population was around 1.....................billion. It more than doubled 2..................... the next 50 years. In the mid-80's, the 3..................... .... slowed. By 2050, the world's population is 4..................... to stabilise at around 9 billion. According to the UN's population division, between 2010 and 2015, around half of the world's people will live in countries with fertility 5..................... of no more than 2.1, the replacement 6..................... of fertility.

只听前40秒

第23题

Plagiarism refers to the copying of an author's language or 1...................

Teachers often find it easy to detect plagiarism because several students have copied a passage from the same 2..................... . Also, students sometimes copy inappropriate information that is unrelated to the 3..................... of the assignment. Institutions may impose different 4..................... for plagiarism depending on how serious the case is. A student may be suspended or 5..................... if a whole piece of writing is found to be copied.

第24题

we are all born with certain physical characteristics determined by our genes

We are all born with certain physical characteristics 1..................... by our genes. But does our DNA 2..................... how we act? Researchers say that genes help control how we 3..................... our environment, but can environment influence which genes are 4..................... ? That leads to debate over the role parents play in 5..................... their children. Some believe the stronger 6..................... influences happen outside the home. As scientists study DNA, they are starting to understand better what makes us 7..................... .

第25题

Traffic in Europe is increasingly 1..................... . The aim of the "European Road Safety Day" is to reduce the 2..................... .... from road accidents throughout the European Union.

The number of lives saved every year since 2001 has 3..................... .... markedly in

line with 4...................... . However, there are still nearly 5...................... people killed on Europe's roads each year.

The big problems to address are speed, alcohol or drugs, and not wearing a 6...................... . These are the 7...................... .... of accidents.

 第26题

Fill the gaps with a maximum of TWO words and/or a number.

For centuries people have been able to improve their lifespans through 1...................... changes. However, a recent study has found that the limits of 2...................... may have already been reached. It is believed that the maximum lifespan may have peaked around the year 3...................... . Researchers concluded that humans can typically live for a maximum of 4...................... years, and that the absolute upper age limit is 5...................... . They recommend that we make efforts to improve the 6...................... of life, rather than to extend life expectancy.

 第27题

WHY IS THE SKY BLUE?

Why is the Sky Blue?

Fill each gap with ONE WORD ONLY.

1 The distance between each .... in a wave of light is called the wavelength.

2 When all the different wavelengths travel together, light appears ....

3 .... light waves have a longer wavelength than blue.

4 The atmosphere is made up of .... which change the way light behaves.

5 Shorter blue light waves .... with particles more often and spread throughout the atmosphere, filling the sky.

6 Other colours pass through and appear .... -white when they mix together.

 第28题

Both anthropologists and archaeologists study the way people live together. Anthropologists study humans' physical, social and 1..................... development, and they 2..................... research by going to locations to ask questions and make 3..................... .

Archaeologists study past societies through their material 4..................... . They recover and examine evidence such as ruins, 5..................... and pottery in order to understand the history, customs and living 6..................... of earlier 7..................... .

These scientists also examine aspects of living societies such as 8..................... differences, physical 9..................... , music or religion. Their field is the wide 10..................... of human social experience.

 第29题

Fill each gap below with ONE WORD ONLY.

South Korea's LG Electronics is 1..................... on its new smart fridge becoming an essential component of kitchens around the world.

The smart fridge is a technological 2..................... compared to fridges of the past. It 3..................... a food management system that maintains a list of the food it is storing. It also records the expiry dates of the foods and sends out an alert 4..................... Wi-Fi when that date has been reached.

The information can be accessed via a 5..................... by consumers as they shop in grocery stores, allowing them to make informed decisions about food purchases. LG adds that its fridge can also suggest healthy 6..................... based on what it knows is inside.

Video games are arguably the best technologically-based teaching 1..................... . When playing a video game, you are an active player who drives the 2..................... and makes decisions that change the 3..................... of what is going on. Psychologists would say that you are learning behavioural 4..................... Video games are 5..................... driven. The medium itself is 6..................... ; we give the valence of good or bad or 7..................... to it. Unfortunately, the most popular video games are the ones that reward you for doing 8..................... against others.

1 The question "Why should I hire you?" gives you the opportunity to restate your .... and summarise your other ....

2 Your answer should be clear, concise and confident, and it should show how your .... relates to your current needs and the problems of the position.

3 Make sure you address some key areas: First determine the company's .... Next show how your skills and .... support the company's needs.

4 Finally, explain how your .... match those given in the company's mission ....

Fill each gap in the following summary with ONE word.

A dissertation is piece of 1..................... research that you do at the end of your university life. It 2..................... upon everything that you have learned so far, and all the skills that you have 3..................... along the way.

These skills include: telling the audience what you have learned, writing in a proper academic 4..................... , as well as putting forward, defending, discussing, 5..................... and concluding an 6..................... .

A dissertation should focus on a 7..................... .... that you select, and that you work on over your last year of study.

第33题

they attempted to achieve their new year's resolutions now :59

The speaker 1...................... the lives of 5000 people as they attempted to achieve their New Year's resolutions. 10% of the people were successful, and they all followed five simple 2...................... First, they broke their goal into a 3...................... of smaller steps. Second, they told friends and family what they were trying to achieve. Third, they regularly 4...................... themselves about the benefits of obtaining their goal. Fourth, they gave themselves a small 5...................... each time they obtained one of their small steps. Finally, they 6...................... .... their progress, so they knew exactly where they were.

第34题

Lecture1: Food in pre-history and the ancient world

- origins of cooked food
- role of cooked food in development of 1......................
- ancient Hebrew 2...................... laws
- cooking and eating in ancient Greece and Rome

Lecture2: Food in the Middle Ages

- the spice 3......................
- changes in the way Europeans cooked, 4...................... and bought food

Lecture3: Food in the Renaissance

- the rise of etiquette and 5......................

- the idea of "magnificence"

- Columbus and food crossing the 6......................

Lecture4: Cooking in France

- nouvelle cuisine

- French 7......................

- the birth of the 8......................

 第35题

The plane has been developed by lots of people 1...................... the years, but the Wright brothers certainly made it work and made it 2...................... . Planes existed before, people had made aeroplanes fly before, but I always have a huge 3...................... for the inventor who really makes it work; Henry Ford I have the same admiration for because he made a car 4...................... , and made it 5......................, and made it work. So the Wright brothers for me are probably the most - should be the most 6...................... people when it comes to aeroplanes.

 第36题

Fill the gaps in the summary using no more than THREE words.

Tip 1: Address the cover letter to a .... person, generally the person in

charge of the department you're applying to or the .... in charge of the interview.

Tip 2: Avoid simply repeating the information in your résumé. Instead, use your cover letter to introduce and highlight your .... , curiosity, and your .... in the field you're applying to work in.

Tip 3: Keep it short, simple and .... , definitely no more than one page, and probably closer to half a page; three paragraphs should do the trick. Resist the .... to ramble on, and instead .... right into the interesting parts.

 第37题

Listen to the recording and fill each gap in the summary with **ONE WORD ONLY.**

Opening or switching a bank account can seem 1...................... , so it's important to start by thinking about why you need a bank account. You may need it in order to receive 2...................... or benefits, to pay 3...................... bills, to take money out of cash 4...................... , or to make payments using a debit card.

Different types of accounts are available. Current accounts are good for 5...................... your day-to-day money. They allow you to go 6...................... , so you'll have to pass a credit check when you apply for one. If you go into the 7...................... you'll have to pay fees and 8...................... . Basic bank accounts are similar to current accounts, but they don't let you go overdrawn.

 第38题

It's impossible to stop spending completely, but you can stop 1...................... spending, or 2...................... it. You really need to set up a 3...................... ; just take a look at how much money you bring home in your 4...................... , and write down everything you spend on a piece of paper. The aim is to get a 5...................... on how much money you are bringing in and where it is going. Whether you use plastic or 6...................... , record what you bought, where you bought it, and how much you 7...................... . At the end of the month it's a real 8...................... . You'll see a whole lot of 9...................... you can do.

<u>How to listen to people effectively</u>

We can use the word **LISTEN** to remind ourselves of the key skills of 1..................... listening.

"L" stands for "look". Look at the person as they are speaking to you, and 2.................. them with good eye contact. "I" stands for "inquire" Use open, 3.................. questions to show interest in the person and what they are saying. "S" reminds you to "4...................." your understanding of what the other person is saying. T 'means "take notes", and "E" means "encourage": smile, 5............... and use .... to encourage them to say more. "N" means "neutralise your feelings": stay 6...................... , avoid .... , and think about the content that the person is trying to 7...................... .... to you.

Summary:

Scientists attach data logging tags to marine 1..................... to measure their movements and behaviour. However, they would like to know whether these tags affect the animals' behaviour or 2.................... consumption.

A research group is currently investigating the effects of drag created by the data logging devices. Dolphins are trained to follow a 3.................... boat while wearing the data logger. The boat is fitted with a 4..................... which records the dolphin's speed and the 5..................... of the session. A trainer then takes breath 6..................... from the dolphin and measures respiratory 7..................... , as well as oxygen and carbon dioxide 8..................... .

In this way, researchers can quantify differences in energy 9..................... when the dolphin is or isn't wearing the data logger.

第41题

Academic libraries are changing faster now than at any time in their history. The 1..................... .... of the library as a physical space housing racks of books and papers is coming under increasing 2..................... . The library stands at a crossroads.

In the digital age, there is an ever-increasing amount of information available to use in a wide 3..................... of different 4..................... and change will be 5..................... by the people that use this information.

While demand for change is coming from users, it is technology that is making it possible to 6..................... this demand. As more and more resources are available on the Internet via search engines, students and researchers now expect to be able to 7..................... information around the clock from almost anywhere in the world and via a growing number of 8....................., from laptops to phones.

Fill the gaps in the summary below with one word only.

I don't think we have a great 1.................. idea of happiness. Many people imagine that happiness comes from something 2.................. ; if you get a new car, a better job, a bigger house, you'll be happy. Whenever I hear the phrase "the 3.................. of happiness", the image that comes to my mind is of racing dogs chasing a mechanical rabbit that's always just out of 4.................... I think a much better goal of life is to be content. Contentment is an inner feeling of satisfaction that's not dependent on external factors. I argue that the goal is to enhance contentment, comfort, serenity and 5.................. so that you can roll with the ups and 6.................. of life and not get thrown off too much. I think it is not realistic to try to be happy all the time; we're 7.................. to be sad or blue some of the time; I think that's part of the 8.................. experience.

 第43题

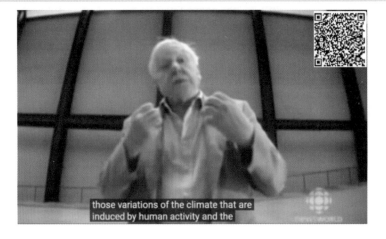

The graph helps us to distinguish between variations in the climate due to 1..................... causes and those variations that are induced by human 2..................... .

The climate is naturally variable. Occasionally there is a downward trend that is associated with a volcano going off. Then we get to a period, from about 1910, where you can start to see an upward trend, a warming of the climate: 3..................... ....

Up to this point, you could argue that climate variation can be explained by natural 4..................... That is no longer the case as you get to the latter part of the 20th century. From about 1970 onwards, you can see the red curve and the green curve beginning to diverge. The yellow curve includes human factors: in particular the 5..................... effect, which is mostly caused by carbon dioxide from 6..................... fuel burning.

There seems little doubt that this steep rise in temperature is due to human activity. Without the action of 7..................... .... , there would have been far less 8..................... change since the 1970's.

第44题

1 Some schools have a .... number of years of required work experience.

2 Stanford applicants should demonstrate examples of ....

3 Some students can .... from their experiences in student politics, clubs, a non- .... organisation or a .... business.

第45题

mm

Two types of PhD:

1 Develop a .... and look for a ....

2 Apply for a project that you have seen ....

Finding an academic to supervise your research proposal:

3 Do a .... on the proposed topic.

4 Or visit the university .... and look at the research interests of staff members.

 第46题

1 Immigration has become a hot political, economic and .... issue.

2 Minorities are creating identities that combine .... of both cultures.

3 Different cultures are coming .... and enriching society.

4 There is no dominant ....

5 It is becoming part of everyday ....

6 I've learnt new languages, and to be more friendly and ....

7 I've learnt how to interact with other cultures and .... them.

The best way to teach people critical thinking, is to teach them to write.

Teaching people to write is extremely 1....................... .... Marking a good essay is easy, but in a bad essay, the words are wrong, the phrases are wrong, the sentences are wrong, the sentence 2....................... is wrong, the paragraphs aren't .... , and the whole thing .... no sense. Students should learn to write well because there is no 3....................... between writing and thinking. Thinking makes you 4....................... effectively in the world and win the battles you 5....................... .

1 Does the amount of .... you have affect the kind of person you are?

2 In a recent study, drivers of luxury cars were three to four times more .... to break the law than drivers of less expensive, low .... cars.

3 The academic paper that resulted .... everywhere.

4 It is very clear that this study of social class touched a ....

5 The results were .... across thirty studies which were run on thousands of people all over the United States.

 第49题

"CORE Principle" coaching

The "C" stood for commitment. We 1...................... people for commitment: have they got an intrinsic 2...................... towards achieving a goal?

The "O" is ownership. We like people to have an opinion, and we 3...................... an environment where people don't feel frightened or under 4...................... to speak their minds.

The "R" is 5...................... (and accountability). People need to understand what they are accountable for, as well as what they are not accountable for.

If you take these elements together, that then 6...................... to the "E", which is 7...................... .

 第50题

Isaac Newton was renowned for his expertise in 1...................., 2...................., 3.................... and theology. His Mathematical Principles of Natural Philosophy was published in 4................... . Newton's first law is named the law of 5...................... .His second law relates to 6......................

His third law states that for every action there is an 7......................and 8......................reaction.

Newton also invented the first 9.....................telescope, he devised the theory of 10.....................,
and he is credited with the invention of the mathematical study known as 11....................... He is
considered to have had one of the greatest scientific 12.....................in history.

 第51题

Paul Allain
Professor of Theatre and Performance

The kind of person who should apply for
a PhD is someone who's got curiosity,

Fill each gap in the summary below with one word only.

If you're thinking of applying for a PhD, you'll need curiosity, 1..................... and dedication.
You also need good academic 2..................... , such as a first class or 2.1 honours degree. You need
a 3..................... for study and for 4..................... work, and you need to be motivated.

It's important that you find a 5..................... who has expertise in your area of interest, and
so you should look at some of the key 6..................... in your chosen field. Find someone who is
doing research related to your field, and make 7..................... with them. They will be involved in
your 8..................... as it develops.

 第52题

Student A(Woman)

University lectures involve everyone on a course 1..................... up and
receiving information from one of the 2..................... about a particular topic.

Seminars, on the other hand, are 3...................... group meetings in which students discuss in detail the 4...................... of ideas that they heard about in a lecture.

Student B(Man)

A university timetable will consist of a 5...................... of lectures and seminars. The number of people in lectures can 6...................... depending on the course. For my course we have about 400 people in a big lecture 7...................... . The number of people attending a small-group seminar 8...................... between 10 and 20.

 第53题

There are more people living in cities than in 1...................... areas. Urbanisation is the defining phenomenon of this century; half of the world's population is urban. Many people are enticed from rural areas by the 2...................... of a better life. We need to improve living conditions for the urban poor by providing adequate 3...................... , clean water and 4...................... .

One key to making cities 5...................... better is good planning. Planners need to 6...................... cities to make them beneficial for all citizens. Cities need green transport and green 7...................... ; they need to be energy 8...................... and pedestrian- 9...................... , with housing and jobs to 10...................... people to come to live there.

 第54题

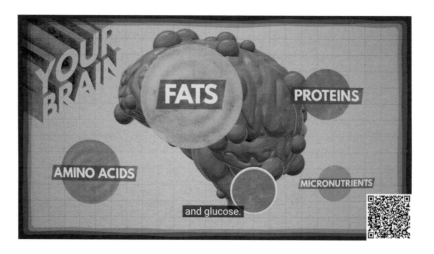

1 The weight of a dehydrated brain comes from from fats, proteins, amino acids, ... micronutrients, and glucose.

2 Omega-rich foods, such as nuts, seeds and fatty fish, are .... the creation and maintenance of cell membranes.

3 Proteins and amino acids affect the way we feel and behave. Neurotransmitters .... that affect mood, sleep, attentiveness and weight.

4 A diet with a range of foods helps maintain a .... of brain messengers, and keeps your mood from getting skewed in one direction or the other.

5 The human brain uses up to 20% of our .... , even though it only accounts for around 2% of our body weight.

 第55题

The Elevator Pitch

A good elevator pitch is made up of two key 1..................... . First, you have to lay out the "2..................... statement": What problem is it that you are trying to solve? Second, you must show the "3..................... proposition": How does your 4..................... solve that problem?

Every great elevator pitch must meet four key tests: First, it must be 5..................... . Second, it must be easy to understand; there's no 6..................... for "tech-talk". Third, it must be greed-inducing; after all, 7..................... want to make money, and lots of it. Finally, it has to be irrefutable; if your elevator pitch leaves investors with more 8..................... than 9..................... , you'd better go back to the 10..................... board.

Are we getting overwhelmed with an always-connected, 1...................... lifestyle, and is that going to lead to less 2...................... thoughts as we move away from the slower, deeper, contemplative state of reading?

The great 3...................... of scientific and technological innovation has been the historic increase in 4...................... , and our ability to reach out and exchange ideas with other people, and to borrow other people's 5...................... and combine them with our 6...................... and turn them into something new. That has been the primary 7...................... of creativity and innovation over the last 600 or 700 years.

It's true we're more 8...................... , but what has happened that is really miraculous and marvelous over the last 15 years is that we have so many new ways to 9...................... and find other people who have that 10...................... piece that will complete the idea we're working on.

选择题技巧

选择题技巧

选择题很多同学觉得难，是因为有大量的阅读内容，独白会把每个选项都提及，不断地否定或肯定。

1 尽量在对白开始之前利用空隙时间去阅读题干和选项；

2 画出每个选项的信号词，这些信号词能够帮助你分区各个选项；

3 在录音播放的时候，不要再读所有内容，把注意力只放在信号词上；

4 小心对白中的陷阱，它们会提及很多题干，先肯定后否定，或先否定再肯定；

5 如果不确定，那就随便猜一个，选择题可千万别空着，然后赶紧听下一题；

6 如果确实没时间读题了，能读几个算几个，并不一定要所有题都做对；

当然，再多的技巧也比不上平时多加练习！

选择题技巧

选择题的一个难点就在各个选项的相似度很高，区别选项成了审题的重要一环。咱们按照以下方式来提升区分技巧：

1 在《雅思听力真题还原》中选一个part的选择题，仔细读题干；

2 看看每个选项之间的区别，并画出一到两个词来区分出题干；

3 反问自己，能否仅凭这几个信号词就区分出题干；

考前备考：

1 平时多练习一些选择题，而且是只练习选择题（比如有填空题也有选择题的题目）

2 你可以使用鸭圈雅思真题库网站来进行专门的听力选择题练习

3 同学们可以尝试这个方法：不看题，直接听录音，听到不清楚的或听不懂的地方就暂停。如果你发现自己都能完全听懂录音，那说明问题可能出现在审题速度太慢或做题技巧；如果录音无法完全听懂，那说明问题还是出在听得不够多。

首先可以在毫无准备的情况下做一part选择题，看看自己做的怎么样；

试着无限次暂停录音，无限次回放，看看自己的正确率如何。如果比平时高，说明问题出在听得不够多不够熟练，如果比平时低，说明问题出在审题。

强制要求自己只允许一个选项画出一个关键词，然后听录音，看看自己能否仅凭这个关键词作对题目。如果比平时高，说明你找的关键词是对的，且能帮助你提升审题效率。

考场技巧：

1 尽量用听力间隙去审题。如果你的听力能力还不错，在part1和part2的做题间隙，也可以提前阅读part3的题干。

2 在每个题干和选项中都画出1~2个信号词，把注意力集中到这几个词上，这能够帮助你更加集中精力。

3 务必要注意同义替换，你不太可能听到和题干、选项中完全相同的词或词组。

4 读题时一定要至少看两道题，防止自己因为走神而跟丢。

5 如果确实跟丢了一道题，不要紧张，赶紧去听下一题的信号词。

Part3 的选择题

有些同学会觉得part4很难，有些同学会觉得part3更难。之所以会有这样的感觉是因为part3都是选择题，主要有以下几个难点：

你既要读题干还要读选项，短时间的阅读量很大；

你的耳朵在听的同时，你的眼睛要定位选项，这提出了更高的要求；

有时候选项是非常近似的，有时候仅仅只有一个单词的区别；

对白有时候会先肯定一个选项，然后立即否定，给你制造陷阱；

画关键词

很多同学会觉得选择题难，因为在录音播放之前要阅读的信息量非常多，不仅有题干还有每个选项。笔者给大家的建议是利用好间隙时间，画出题干和选项的关键词，像这样：

31 According to the speaker, how might a guest feel when staying in a luxury hotel?

A impressed with the facilities　　　留心关于客户感受，感想的信息

B depressed by the experience

C concerned at the high costs　笔者画出了三个形容词对三个选项进行了区分

32 According to recent research, luxury hotels overlook the need to

A provide for the demands of important guests　他们忽视了什么？留心关于酒店做错了什么的信息

B create a comfortable environment

C offer an individual and personal welcome　笔者画出了具体的内容，A是贵客需求，B是舒适环境，C是客人迎接

33 The company focused their research on

A a wide variety of hotels　　他们关注什么类型的酒店呢？

B large, luxury hotel chains

C exotic holiday hotels 笔者圈出了三个形容词加以区分

34 What is the impact of the outside environment on a hotel guest?

A It has a considerable effect　　影响的程度如何？

B It has a very limited effect

C It has no effect whatsoever 笔者画出了三个形容词加以区分，A是巨大，B是很小，C是没有

词汇对于选择题的重要性

一些学生会觉得下面的题很难，是因为独白的词汇。

1 Joanna concentrated on women performers because

A women are more influenced by fashion.

B women's dress has led to more controversy.

C women's code of dress is less strict than men's.

2 Frost's article suggests that in popular music, women's dress is affected by

A their wish to be taken seriously.

B their tendency to copy each other.

C their reaction to the masculine nature of the music.

听力原文：

You only had women performers in your study. Was that because male musicians are less worried about fashion?

I think a lot of the (A)men are very much influenced by fashion, but in social terms (C)the choices they have are more limited...they'd really upset audiences if they strayed away from quite narrow boundaries.

远离   有限选择

这道题最关键的破题点就是最后这几个单词，strayed away from quite narrow boundaries其实就是less strict的同义词组；而如果你听不懂narrow boundaries的话，这道题就很难选对。本题答案为C。

随意穿着

Frost points out that a lot of female singers and musicians in popular music tend to dress down in performances, (C)and wear less feminine clothes, like jeans instead of skirts, and he suggests this is (A) because otherwise they'd just be discounted as trivial.

不重视   不重要的

这道题也有两个关键词组，C选项的masculine nature对应原文的less feminine clothes，但请注意，C选项说的是她们的中性穿着是对中性音乐的反映，但实际上是d

第一题的答案是C，第二题的答案是A，

画关键词

这道题也有两个关键词组，C选项的masculine nature对应原文的less feminine clothes，请注意，C选项说的是她们的中性穿着是对中性音乐的反映，但实际上第一题的答案是C，第二题的答案是A。也就是那些在听的时候需要额外留意的词。咱们来看这道题，看看你画的跟笔者是否一致。（请注意，画关键词并没有标准答案）

1 How will Rosie and Martin introduce their presentation?

A with a drawing of woolly mammoths in their natural habitat

B with a timeline showing when woolly mammoths lived

C with a video clip about woolly mammoths

2 What was surprising about the mammoth tooth found by Russell Graham?

A It was still embedded in the mammoth's jawbone.

B It was from an unknown species of mammoth.

C It was not as old as mammoth remains from elsewhere.

（《剑桥雅思真题14》）

千万不要画那些在很多题干重复的单词，比如上文的mammoth，它起不到信号的作用。（频繁出现的词不能成为信号词）应该更多的画出区别于各个选项的词。带着这些信号词，咱们来看一下原文：

Martin: We thought we needed something general about woolly mammoths in our introduction, to establish that they were related to our modern elephant, and they lived thousands of years ago in the last ice age.

Rosie: (C)Maybe we could show a video clip of a cartoon about mammoths. But that'd be a bit childish. Or (B)we could have a diagram, it could be a timeline to show when they lived, with illustrations?
幼稚的

Martin: (A)Or we could just show a drawing of them walking in the ice? No, let's go with your last suggestion.

Tutor: Good. Then you're describing the discovery of the mammoth tooth on St Paul's Island in Alaska, and why it was significant.

Rosie: Yes. The tooth was found by a man called Russell Graham. He picked it up from under a rock in a cave. He knew it was special - for a start it was in really good condition, as if (A)it had been just extracted from the animal's jawbone. Anyway, they found it was 6,500 years old.
下颌骨

Tutor: So why was that significant?

Rosie: Well, (C)the mammoth bones previously found on the North American mainland were much less recent than that. So this was really amazing.

根据原文，不难得出第一题的答案是B，第二题的答案是C。你可以看到信号词对于学生破题起到了关键性的定位作用。

选择题

选择题有时候会很难，因为对话会涉及所有选项，学生来看这道题：

Janice thinks that employers should encourage workers who are

A potential leaders.

B open to new ideas.

C good at teamwork.

（《剑桥雅思真题7》Page15）

下面是Janice的谈话：

"Well, currently teamwork is in fashion in the workplace and in my opinion the importance of the individual is generally neglected. What managers should be targeting is those employees who can take the lead in a situation and are not afraid to accept the idea of responsibility."

可以很清楚的看到，所有的选项都被提及了。所以你并不能够听到什么就选什么。从原文中不难读出该题选A，但如果是听出来就有点难了。

选择题难题

很多同学会觉得听力选择题有些难，主要是因为：选项很多，听力的时候要特别认真；有些选项还很类似；几乎所有选项都会被提及；有些选项在听力原文中是以同义词形式出现的（非原词）

咱们来看这道题：

Which TWO facilities at the leisure club have recently been improved?

A the gym

B the tracks

C the outdoor pool

D the indoor pool

E the sports training for children

（《剑桥雅思真题10》Page12）

C和D是两个很类似的选项，

Which two answers did you choose? Did you experience any of the four difficulties that I mentioned above?

CORRECT ANSWERS FROM SIMON:

D

we've expanded it to 8 lanes

(there isn't space for an outdoor pool)

A

recently refurbished fitness suite

多选题

What decision has not yet been made about the pool?

A whose statue will be at the door

B the exact opening times

C who will open it

（《剑桥雅思真题10》Page35）

原文：

We're on schedule for a June 15th opening date and well within budget. We have engaged award-winning actress Coral White to declare the pool open and there'll be drinks and snacks available at the pool side. There'll also be a competition for the public to decide on the sculpture we plan to have at the entrance; you will decide which famous historical figure from the city we should have.

根据原文，你能找出正确答案吗？哪个关键词帮助你得出答案呢？你能看出每个选项都被提及了吗？

答案是A；

光靠同义词替换还不行

1 Why does Marco's tutor advise him avoid the Team Management course?

A It will repeat work that Marco has already done.

B It is intended for students at a lower level than Marco.

C It may take too much time to do well.

2 Why does Marco want to do a dissertation?

A He thinks it will help his future career.

B He would like to do a detailed study.

C He has already done some work for it

（《Official IELTS Practice Materials 2》）

听力原文：

Tutor: The trouble is that because of changes in the content of various courses, Team Management (A)overlaps with the Introduction to Management course you took in your first year.

　　　　　　重叠

So what you'd learn from it would be too little for the amount of time you'd have to spend on it.

Marco: I'll drop that idea then. Have you had a chance to look at the outline of my finance dissertation?

这道题为什么难？首先是overlaps这个词，如果你听不懂，或者不知道它的同义词是repeat；可能就不会选A；其次是有些同学听到too little可能就选了B，听到time就选了C；其实这就是没听懂的具体表现，听到什么就选什么是不能做对题的，必须听懂。这道题选A。

Tutor: Yes. Why exactly do you want to write a dissertation?

Marco: Well, I'm quite prepared to do the extra work, because I'm keen to investigate something in depth, instead of just skating across the surface. I realise that a broader knowledge base may be more useful to my career, but I'm really keen to do this.

这道题其实有两组同义替换，A题干中的help his future career与原文中的more useful to my career，B选项的do a detailed study与原文中的investigate something in depth；这道题的破局点在but，因为but后面的内容才是答案，选B。

选择题转配对题

其实配对题是选择题的一个变种。下面这个配对题有点难，大家做做看。

What do the students decide about each topic for the presentation?
A They will definitely include this topic.
B They might include this topic.
C They will not include this topic.

1 Geographical Location ....
2 Economy ....
3 Overview of Education System ....
4 Role of English Language ....

听力原文：

A:OK...but I think we ought to say something about the geographical location...cos not a lot of people know where the islands are...

B:Yes...OK...I'll take notes, shall I?

A:Yeah, that'll be a help...

B:So, geographical location...

A:Then we ought to give an overview of the whole education system.

B:Shouldn't we say something about the economy...you know

A:agricultural produce...minerals and so forth?

B:Well...Dr.White said we shouldn't go into that sort of detail.

A:But it's pretty important when you think about it...you know

B:because it does influence the education system...

A:Look...let's think about that one later shall we? Let's see how we're doing for time...

B:OK...so...general overview of education

A:Of course...and then the role of English language...

B:Nope...that goes in the Language Policy Seminar...don't you remember?

对于配对题来说，题干的词原文中通常都是以原词出现的，是完美的信号词。第1题 Geographical Location，ought to say 是 definitely 的同义词，选A；第三题 Overview of Education System，ought to give 是 definitely 的同义词，选A；第2题 Economy，think about that one later 是 might include 的同义词，选B；第4题 the role of English language，nope 很明显和 not include 的同义词，选C；这道题的难题应该是在第2和第3题，因为信号词出现的顺序和题目顺序是不同的，原文进行了反复陈述。

分辨迷惑选项

The exact proportion of land devoted to private gardens was confirmed by

A consulting some official documents

B taking large-scale photos

C discussions with town surveyors

（《剑桥雅思真题9》Page85）

听力原文：

The first thing we did was to establish what proportion of the urban land is taken up by private gardens. We estimated that it was about one fifth, and this was endorsed by looking at large-scale usage maps in the town land survey office.

这道题非常有难度，首先信号词 confirmed by 的同义词 endorsed by（被认可）很多同学不一定能分辨出来。其次，题干中的关键词（或其同义词）都被提及了，需要考生去排除：**B选项**，原文虽然有 large-scale，但并没有 taking...photos；C选项，原文虽然有 town surveyors，但并没有 discussions；**A选项**是正确的，official documents 指代的就是 maps。

画出选项中的关键词

对于选择题来说，趁着听力对白间隙，学生需要在选项上画一些关键词来区分选项，这会有效减少学生的审题时间。请看下面的例题：

What helped Rob to prepare to play the character of a doctor?

A the stories his grandfather told him

B the times when he watched his grandfather working

C the way he imagined his grandfather at work

画关键词并没有什么铁律，画的目的仅仅只是为了区别不同的选项，学生需要选取那些最大程度能够代表整个选项大意的词或词组。这道题三个选项都是关于grandfather的，所以grandfather肯定不能作为区分词。A选项可以圈出stories，是关于一个故事的；（当然，如果你圈出told这个动词也是可以的）B选项和C选项其实非常接近，不过一个是watched，一个是imagined。其实有经验的考生大概率会猜到，正确答案应该在B和C之间，而且考点就是watched或imagined。

听力原文：

I have to write about the role I played, the doctor, how I developed the character. My grandfather was a doctor before he retired, and I just based it on him. He must have all sorts of stories, but he never says much about his work. I'd visualise what he must have been like in the past, when he was sitting in his consulting room listening to his patients.

这道题的考点就在visualise，它到底是看见还是想象呢？假设你不认识这个词，但后面的what he must have been like in the past也告诉学生了，Rob是imagined而不是watched，**正确选项是C**。

画哪些关键词？

1 What will be the main topic of Trudie and Stewart's paper?

A how public library services are organised in different countries

B how changes in society are reflected in public libraries

C how the funding of public libraries has changed

2 They agree that one disadvantage of free digitalised books is that

A they may take a long time to read

B they can be difficult to read

C they are generally old

（《剑桥雅思真题12》）

解析：

拿到题目，是两个同学关于paper的讨论，第1题题干的关键词肯定是the main topic，三个选项都有public library，说明接下来的对话是围绕public library的，但它肯定不适合做信号词，因为出现太频繁，笔者分别画出了organised in different countries/changes in society/the funding这三个信号词。

听力原文：

(**Trudie**) Maybe we should concentrate on this country, and try to relate the changes in libraries to external developments, like the fact that more people can read than a century ago..... We're only supposed to write a short paper, so it's probably best if we don't go into funding in any detail.

第1题 A选项，原文说的是this country,不是题干说的different countries，排除；**B选项**，原文的external developments是changes in society的同义词组，正确；C选项，通过the funding定位，原文却说if we don't go into funding in any detail，排除；

第2题的讨论主题肯定是围绕free digitalised books的，笔者画出的关键词是disadvantages，学生需要听到一个关于free digitalised books的缺点。三个选项各画出一个形容词，take a long time/ difficult/ generally old，期待在听力原文中听到它们三个的同义词。

听力原文：

(Stewart) But the digitalised books that are available online for free are mostly out of copyright, aren't they? And copyright in this country lasts for 70 years after the author dies. So you won't find the latest best-seller or up-to-date information..... (**Trudie**) That's an important point.

第2题 A和B选项，原文没有提及；C选项中的generally old和听力原文中的won't find up-to-date information是同义词组，正确；

听力关键词

笔者经常在阅读中强调找关键词，其实听力考试中也是一样。先读题干，然后再仔细听录音，看看能不能听出来信号词或信号词的同义词。咱们来看下面这个题：

1 The course takes place on

A Monday, Wednesday and Friday

B Monday, Tuesday and Wednesday

C Monday, Thursday and Friday

2 Which argument was used *against* having a drama theatre?

A It would be expensive and no students would use it

B It would be a poor use of resources and only a minority would use it

C It could not accommodate large productions of plays

（《剑桥雅思真题4》Test3）

第1题，三个选项都有Monday，显然它不能作为关键词；A和B选项都有Wednesday，所以真正能区分选项的是A选项的Wednesday，B选项的Tuesday和C选项的Thursday。第2题问的是为什么反对剧院，选项给出了三种不同的理由，学生所圈出的信号词一定要能够代表这个选项，所以笔者选择了三个形容词（组），分别是：expensive,poor use of resources和not accommodate。

多选题划分题干

Which **TWO** things can make the job of kitchen assistant stressful?

A They have to follow orders immediately

B The kitchen gets very hot

C They may not be able to take a break

D They have to do overtime

E The work is physically demanding

（《剑桥雅思真题12》Test5-Section2）

拿到这个题目，你会画哪些关键词以区分选项呢？首先是题干，哪两件事让帮厨的人stressful？A选项说帮厨们需要立即follow orders；B选项说厨房非常hot；C选项说他们可以take a break；D选项说他们必须overtime；E选项说他们的工作physically demanding；其实无论是名词，动词还是形容词，只要是代表这个选项大意的词，或是能区别于其他选项的词，都可以做关键词。

画完关键词，学生来看原文：

　　Now, you may have heard that this can be a stressful job, and I have to say that can be true. You'll be working an eight-hour day for the first week, though you'll have the chance to do overtime after that as well if you want to. But however long the hours are, you'll get a break in the middle. What you will find is that you're on your feet all day long, lifting and carrying, so if you're not fit now you soon will be! You'll find you don't have much chance to take it easy - when someone tells you to do something, you need to do it straightaway - but at least we do have a very efficient air conditioning system compared with some kitchens.

　　当学生听到stressful时知道进入答案区域，并且学生也听到了D选项中的overtime和C选项中的get a break，但实际真正的答案出现在What you will find it that之后，因为后面才是真正的理由。通常情况，原文不会直接出现选项中的关键词的原词（那对大家来说太简单啦），一般是以同义替换形式出现。E选项中的physically demanding和you're on your feet all day long是同义词组；A选项中的follow orders和when someone tells you to do something是同义词组；B选项与原文we do have a very efficient air conditioning system相反，厨房不热，所以答案为A和E。

Which TWO things surprised the students about the traffic-light system for nutritional labels?

A its widespread use

B the fact that it is voluntary for supermarkets

C how little research was done before its introduction

D its unpopularity with food manufacturers

E the way that certain colours are used

　　在题干中学生需要画出来surprised，要听出来学生对哪两件事surprised。这里肯定不能画traffic-light system for nutritional labels。

听力原文：

What do you think of the traffic-light system?

I think supermarkets like the idea of (E)having a colour-coded system-red, orange or green-for levels of fat, sugar and salt in a product.But (A)it's not been adopted universally. And not on all products. Why do you suppose that is?

Pressure from the food manufacturers. Hardly surprising that some of them are opposed to flagging up how unhealthy their products are.

引起……的注意

(B)I'd have thought it would have been compulsory. It seems ridiculous it isn't.

必修的

I know. (C)And what I couldn't get over is the fact that it was brought in without enough consultation-a lot of experts had deep reservations about it.

第一题的答案是B，第二题的答案是C。

选择题练习

第1题

What is Brian going to do before the course starts?

A attend a class

B write a report

C read a book

第2题

1 Which 3D printed product can already be bought?

A computers

B glasses

C mobile phones

2 Which **THREE** materials can be used in 3D printers?

A paper

B metal

C wood

D glass

E concrete

第3题

1 What TWO things will the examiner do before the test?

A Ask for a paper driving licence

B Check your paperwork

C Speak to your driving instructor

D Give you the option of bringing your driving instructor with you

E Give you and your instructor some feedback

2 Which **TWO** of the following statements are true of the test?

A An eyesight check is not part of the test

B You can ask the examiner questions about safety

C You have to drive in a variety of traffic conditions

D The test lasts about 10 minutes

E You will be asked to follow signs or spoken instructions

第4题

1 The original buildings on the site were

A houses

B industrial buildings

C shops

2 The local residents wanted to use the site for

A leisure

B apartment blocks

C a sports centre

 第5题

Which TWO facilities at the leisure club have recently been improved?

A the gym

B the tracks

C the outdoor pool

D the indoor pool

E the sports training for children

(《剑桥雅思真题10》Page12)

 第6题

1 How does the first speaker describe multitasking?

A it is a myth

B it is efficient but distracting

C it reduces the time that tasks take

2 Which **TWO** statements are true according to the second speaker?

A people who can multitask are more effective

B people should always focus on one thing only

C we need permission to get things done

D the brain is less productive when we are distracted

E organisations are unproductive if they are constantly on-line

 第7题

Which TWO of the statements below agree with the speaker's advice?

How to establish a routine for your toddler:

A This is an easy task for most parents.

B The parent must establish a routine before expecting the child to follow one.

C Busy parents need help with their children.

D Parents should include the child's sleep times in their schedules.

E Meal times don't need to be included in parents' plans.

 第8题

1 Which website are you advised to use when paying for your ticket?

A the East Coast website

B Thetrainline.com

C the Ticket Alert website

2 Which **TWO** statements are true of the East Coast website?

A You pay a £1.50 booking fee.

B It can only be used for booking trains from London to Edinburgh.

C You can use it to buy train tickets for anywhere in the UK.

D You will not be charged for using a credit card.

E You can buy a "Super Advance" ticket the night before your trip.

 第9题

1 Many teachers believe that

A plagiarism is not a big problem

B too many students are guilty of plagiarism

C many students copy each other's essays

2 Plagiarism is a problem because

A a student's true level of ability will not be known

B students have to rewrite their essays

C many students do not get caught

3 Teachers can spot plagiarism by

A using free software

B comparing different students' writing styles

C putting key words into a search engine

 第10题

Which **THREE** of these statements are true?

A The smart fridge is an essential component of kitchens.

B It is technologically advanced in comparison with other fridges.

C It alerts users when foods reach their expiry date.

D It can help consumers when they are out shopping.

E It is able to make decisions about food purchases.

F It can tell users which foods are healthier.

第11题

Which **THREE** things is the speaker going to talk about?

A how to achieve your goals

B how to waste time

C how to deal with your boss

D how to deal with your advisor

E how to delegate

F how to cope with stress

Which TWO things should students do when applying to the course?

A Understand what the course is about.

B Think carefully about what they can contribute to the course.

C Tell a story about an experience that they have had.

D Provide a large quantity of work that shows their ability.

E Show an example of their own film work if possible.

F Explain why they are interested in the course.

Choose **THREE** characteristics of effective teachers from the list below.

A They use the largest number of exercises

B They know how to choose examples

C They pick the right technique at the right moment

D Being older can be an advantage

E They are chess players

F They pay more attention to students

1 What are the TWO main reasons why students have trouble remembering information for tests?

A stress

B nerves

C lack of time in the test

D lack of planning

E lack of preparation

2 Which **TWO** relaxation techniques are **NOT** recommended by the speaker?

A breathing deeply

B counting backwards

C closing your eyes

D visualising a relaxing image

E counting slowly

3 Which **TWO** habits can parents help their children with?

A eating properly and getting enough sleep

B organising their study schedules

C buying the right study guide

D breaking the exam down

E cramming

 第15题

1 The speaker states that

A speaking a language is a critical skill

B babies are language learning geniuses

C adults cannot learn a new language

2 The speaker's tests on babies involve

A training them to respond to a sound change

B training them to recognise the sounds of all languages

C training them to respond to a panda bear

3 The speaker describes babies as 'citizens of the world' because

A they understand everything they hear

B they can recognise the difference between the sounds of any language

C their listening skills are as good as adults' listening skills

1 A year from now, the unemployment rate will be

A fairly good

B not as high in California

C very high for the country as a whole

2 One problem is that

A employees cannot work for more than 33 hours per week

B employers will extend working hours instead of hiring new staff

C there are too many part-time workers

3 If the economy begins to improve

A more people will be discouraged from looking for work

B people will think that there are more job opportunities

C there will be an expansion of the workforce

1 What is the probability of right-handed parents having a left-handed child?

A more than 10%.

B about 2%.

C about 17%.

2 What comparison is made between males and females?

A 50% of left-handed people are male.

B Males are less likely to be left-handed.

C Males are twice as likely to be left-handed.

3 A child's handedness can be determined for certain

A when the child reaches two years of age.

B when the child is six months old.

C according to which hand the child reaches with in the first year of life.

1 What subject does Professor Wigen usually teach?

A Geography

B Japanese history

C Map-making

2 What will be covered in this particular class?

A The history and variety of maps

B A focus on the most unusual maps

C The career of famous map-makers

3 Who will teach the course?

A The lecturer alone

B The lecturer and artists on the web

C The lecturer and perhaps some other speakers

4 What does the final assignment involve?

A Creating a series of questions about a selection of maps

B Working with other students to collect interesting maps

C Analysing maps that the lecturer has chosen

原文与解析

1. unable to talk   2. ignore; catch up   3. general development   4. tongue; mouth

(1) Parents start worrying about delayed language development when their child turns two but is still **unable to talk**. He or she may be saying a few words occasionally but is quite behind other children of the same age. If the parents do not notice slowness in any other activities, **(2)**they tend to **ignore** this problem with the hope that their child will soon **catch up**. There are several factors

one reason

that can lead to delay in the course of language development. **(3)**It could be a case of a delay in the **general development** of the child. On the other hand, if the overall development of the child is normal, but there is delay in he's or her language learning skills, **(4)**it may be that the problem is related to the **tongue** or roof of the **mouth**.

caused by

1. notch   2. diversity   3. improved   4. districts   5. facade   6. spirit   7. opportunities   8. hub
9. ease   10. outdoors

这道题的信号词都没有做任何的同意替换，notch和facade的拼写可能会难倒一些同学。

These are the 10 most liveable cities in the world, according to monocle.com.

Number 10, Stockholm: **(1-2)**Top-**notch** education and welfare, but needs more integration for immigrants to increase **diversity**.

Number 9 is Auckland:hosted the Rugby World Cup did wonders, motivating it to create two new entertainment precincts **(3)**and public transport greatly **improved**.

Number 8 is Sydney:**(4)**Innovative mixed use **districts** incorporating cycle paths, verticle gardens are one way the Australian waterside giant is becoming more sophisticated. The central park complex is a triumph in green architecture that can serve as an example for the rest of the world.

Number 7 is Tokyo:**(5-7)hidden under the facade** of a neon-lit mega city is a **small town spirit** featuring **world class shopping and business opportunities**.

Number 6 is Melbourne: **(8-9)Australia's cultural hub** is getting eve better with **a big push to ease** traffic congestion.

Number 5 is Munich: Unemployment is low, but failure to act on a few key projects has hurt Munich's standing. Its airport needs a third runway to compete with the other global cities on this list.

Number 4 is Vienna: continues to evolve from a beautiful relic to a modernized classic. Affordable housing and an imminent brand new campus for the Vienna University's school for economics and business will inject youth into the city.

Number 3 is Copenhagen: the danes are the happiest people on earth because of places like this, **(10)with near-perfect integration between city life** and the **outdoors**. The city aims to be carbon neutral by 2025.

 第3题

1. 1889　2. 1888　3. simple; low-priced　4. 100

请注意，第三题第2个空格只能填low-priced而不能填 relatively low-priced，因为题目只给了一个空格。

The use of photographic film was pioneered by George **Eastman**, who **started manufacturing** paper film in 1885, before switching to **celluloid in 1889**. His first camera, which he called the **Kodak**, was offered for sale in **1888**. It was a very **simple** and relatively **low-priced** box camera aimed at the
was available to consumers
average consumer. The Kodak came with enough film for **a hundred** exposures and needed to be sent
　　normal people　　　　　　　　　　　　　　　　able to take
back to the factory for processing when the roll was finished.

第4题

1. two weeks / 2 weeks 2. email / e-mail 3. alternative date 4. main library building 5. three / 3

Students who would like to visit the university should check the list of visiting days on our website

minimum

to select a convenient date. **(1)**Please remember we need at least **two weeks**' notice to arrange your visit. If you have problems completing the online booking form, **(2)**you may send a copy to us by post, fax or as an **email** attachment. You will be asked to choose two possible visiting days. In this way, if bookings for your first choice exceed a certain level, **(3)**the university will offer you the

on arrival

alternative date stated on your booking form. **(4)**On the day of your visit, prospective students should arrive at the university between 9 and 9. 15am. Please go directly to the **main library building**. Students are encouraged to attend with their parents. **(5)**Although two guests is the normal limit, you may bring an extra person if you inform us in writing beforehand. On our busier visiting days,

预先

guests and parents will unfortunately be unable to visit academic departments.

第5题

1. disorganised/disorganized 2. too much, interest 3. mistakes 4. trying to hide 5. the worst

Common mistakes people make when writing **(1)**a CV include having a **disorganized** CV without any structure. Your CV should be like a good story with a beginning, middle and end to keep the reader interested. **(2)**Writing **too much** with long paragraphs or sentences is guaranteed to lose people's **interest** very quickly and end up on the no pile. Misspelling or poor grammar shouldn't be a problem for anyone these days. Use your computer's spellchecker or simply get a friend or family member to check it for you, as **(3)**its often really hard to spot your own **mistakes**. **(4)**Unexplained gaps and the dates on your CV's will raise questions from a recruiter, not only about your ability to be accurate but also about what you might be **trying to hide**. A six month period that isn't accounted for on your CV may simply be a typing error but **(5)**it could have a potential employer thinking **the worse**.

cause

第6题

1. tuition tourism　2. applicants　3. doubled　4. fees

Many leave home to study. And for some that doesn't just mean another city, it can mean another country. Amsterdam is one of the places **(Q1)**that's becoming increasingly popular as a destination for a sort of **tuition tourism**. At Amsterdam University College you can study in English. **(2)**This is one of the courses deliberately designed to attract **applicants** from all over the world including the UK. At the start of this month, Emily left Colchester to begin a degree here. And several Dutch colleges want others to follow that path. The Holland here at the University of Amsterdam, **(3)**there's still a relatively small number of **British students**, but the amount is **doubled** between last year and this. **(4)**And they expect the numbers to increase considerably when **tuition fees** rise in the UK next year.

 第7题

1. voluntary　2. compulsory　3. charity　4. roadside　5. tutoring　6. raising

7. high school diploma　8. contributed

(1-2) Community service is the practice of **voluntary** or **compulsory** unpaid work within a community. Examples of community service projects include cleaning a park, **(3-4)**collecting items for **charity** such as clothes, food or furniture, cleaning **roadside** verges, helping the elderly and nursing homes, helping the local fire or police service, helping out at a local library, **(5-6)tutoring** children with learning disabilities or **raising** money for projects in the local area. In many areas of the United States, a certain number of hours of community service is required to graduate from high school. In some high schools in Washington state for example, **(7)**students must complete 60 hours of **community service** to receive a **high school diploma**. Some Washington school districts have differentiated between community service and **(8)**service learning which requires students to demonstrate that **their work** has **contributed** to their education.

show

 第8题

1. access to information　2. shift in demand　3. adapt our skills　4. digital world

公平的

The libraries of the future are still about equitable **access to information** for our communities and our customers. However, what we do know is that, we now have a 10% **shift in demand** from traditional print material into the electronic world. So we've got to move to more digital faster. But that requires a balance: we're not throwing out the print, but we need to **adapt our skills** to work within this **digital world**. It's a really exciting time to be a librarian, as we adapt to this changing way our customers are using information.

 第9题

1. put on   2. step further; goes into   3. drastically reduce; second-hand   4. picking up; light up

Over the last decade smokers across the country have been **put on** the defensive. New York City is now taking the war against tobacco a **step further** with a new law that **goes into** effect tomorrow, banning smoking outdoors. The law aims to **drastically reduce** , if not eliminate, exposure to **second-hand** smoke.

Officials also hope to discourage a new generation from **picking up** the habit, sending out the message that it is no longer acceptable to **light up** in family-friendly places.

 第10题

1 I work in the **healthcare** field, and have always wanted to go abroad and offer my **services**.

2 I guess I just wanted to do volunteer work cause I wanted to do something **different**: travel around but, like, really see the people, you know, rather than just being a **visitor**.

3 Here you're in a safe **environment**, where you're looked after, and all the **staff** are really friendly.

4 They really want you to grasp the **culture** that you're coming into, and the people that surround you, and just everything: the way that they live, their everyday lives.

5 If you're willing to give the time and the energy, I think it can be an amazing **opportunity**, and you can learn so much.

6 There's more than just, you know, reading a **guide** book and going to the tourist **spots**. It's about sitting down and trying to communicate with people and trying to understand what their experiences are.

 第11题

1. frequent reason   2. authority   3. desire to make   4. digital media   5. everyday lifestyle
6. values of community

Beginning in the 1990s, the most **frequent reason** given for attending college had changed from reasons such as becoming an **authority** in a field or helping others to the **desire to make** a lot of money. At the same time, compact disc players, **digital media**, personal computers, and cellular telephones all began to integrate into **everyday lifestyle**. Madeline Levine criticised what she saw as a large change in American culture – "a shift away from **values of community**, spirituality, and integrity, and toward competition, materialism and disconnection."

 第12题

1.chief good   2. valuable   3. objective   4. dramatically   5. explosion   6. gender   7. marriage

So, people want a lot of things out of life, but I think, more than anything else, they want happiness. **(1)Aristotle called happiness** "the **chief good**," the end towards which all other things aim.
　　　　　　亚里士多德　　　　　　　　　　首善
According to this view, the reason we want a big house or a nice car or a good job. **(2)Isn't that these things are intrinsically valuable**. It's that we expect them to bring us happiness. Now, in the last 50
　　　　　从本质上来说
years, we Americans have gotten a lot of the things that we want. We're richer. We live longer. We have access to technology that would have seemed like science fiction just a few years ago. **(3-4) The paradox of happiness** is that even though the **objective** conditions of our lives have improved

dramatically, we haven't actually gotten any happier. Maybe because these conventional notions of

传统观念

progress haven't delivered big benefits in terms of happiness, there's been an increased interest in recent years in happiness itself. People have been debating the causes of happiness for a really long time. In fact, for thousands of years, but it seems like many of those debates remain unresolved.

尚未解答的

Well, as with many other domains in life, I think the scientific method has the potential to answer this question. In fact, **(5)**in the last few years, there's been an **explosion** in research on happiness. For example, **(6-7)**we've learned a lot about its demographics, how things like income and **education**,

人口统计数据

gender and **marriage** relate to it. But one of the puzzles this has revealed is that factors like these don't seem to have a particularly strong effect.

 第13题

1. course 2. deal 3. pride 4. welcome 5. responsibility 6. element 7. package 8. ends

地方政府

(1) But over the **course** of this last weekend, the local authority here say they collected twenty tonnes of rubbish from this beach. "Well let's talk to the leader of the local council here in Brighton Jason Kick. Alright Jason, twenty tonnes seems like an extraordinary amount to me. Is that normal?"

令人惊奇的

"It is for a summer weekend unfortunately. **(2-5)**It costs us a great **deal** of money to collect that but obviously we take **pride** in our beach and we want to **welcome** visitors but I would hope that

引以为豪的

people take **responsibility** for their rubbish and we would take out lots and lots of bins on a weekend particularly and unfortunately people aren't making use of them always. " "Is it just irresponsible behavior? I mean are there enough bins? Do you help people enough?" "I think there are a huge

不负责任的行为

number of bins, if we put any more out on the weekend there wouldn't be anywhere for people to lie down so **(6-8)**I think there is an **element** of responsibility here but also the suppliers need to think about how they **package** their goods and we need to attack this problem at both **ends**. "

从两方面来解决这个问题

第14题

1. foremost 2. context 3. history 4. community 5. unlike 6. voices 7. critical 8. contexts

John Dewey was America's **foremost** philosopher and philosopher of education. His ideas are important to education today because he recognised that each individual brings a certain **context** and **history** to his or her learning. He also understood the importance of learning in a group or **community**, learning from others that are **unlike** you. The essence of a democracy is that you have different **voices** and you learn from each of them, and Dewey celebrated that. He would probably be **critical** of the current system of education because it ignores the teaching **contexts** and what each student brings to the classroom.

 第15题

1. lefty 2. being 3. start 4. toddler

It turns out that more than 10% of people, or about 10%, are left-handed. If both parents are right-handed, there's about a 2% chance your child is going to be a **lefty**. If one parent is left-handed, it's about 17%, and if both parents are lefties, there's about a 50% chance your child is also going to be left-handed, with guys **being** twice as often left-handed as girls.

So how do you tell what your child is going to be? Well, when your baby is about six months of age, he or she may **start** to reach with their right hand, but very quickly will bring out their left hand, and it's not until a baby or a **toddler** is two years of age that we can really determine hand preference.

第16题

1. myth 2. founder 3. fallacy 4. network 5. mode

(1) The fact is, multitasking is a **myth**. Our brains can't do it. You simply become less efficient and more distracted, your error rate goes up 50 percent, and it takes you twice as long to do the same task. Listen what Tim Jenkins has to say. **(2)**He's the co-**founder** of **Point B**, a leading business consulting firm. **(3)** "Well, I think there's a **fallacy** out there, that folks that can multitask are more effective. There

谬论

are times when it's just important to focus on one thing. I think we also need to give people permission to check out, **(4)**to check out of the communications **network** temporarily to get things done; because when you're always on, when you're always online, you're always distracted, right, **(5)**and the brain really is telling us that is a very unproductive **mode** to be in. So the always online organisation is actually the always unproductive organisation."

第17题

1. preferably 2. alert 3. sell out 4. pop 5. quid (a'quid' is one British pound (£ 1) in informal British English) 6. way 7. worth

(1) The first thing any regular train user should do is to book their tickets in advance, **preferably** exactly 12 weeks in advance. Those £300 tickets to Manchester, you can get them for just £25 return if you go online. You go to a website called **Thetrainline.com**, **(2)**you fill in their ticket **alert** system, and you'll get an email telling you when those tickets are available. **(3)**Because they often **sell out** very quickly, so when you get that email, act straight away. But, and I know this sounds a bit sneaky, don't actually buy them on **Thetrainline.com**, because you'll have to pay a £1.50 booking fee, and if you're using your credit card another £1.50. **(4)**Instead, **pop** over to the East

去 ...一下

Coast website - you'd think that's only trains down the East coast from London up to Edinburgh - it's not; they will sell tickets for any trains anywhere in the UK, and they don't charge a booking fee, and they don't charge for credit card. **(5)**So that's another two or three **quid** saved. **(6)**If you haven't been able to buy a ticket a long **way** in advance, it is still worth remembering that up until 6 o'clock on the night before, you can still get Advance tickets. They won't be as cheap as the Super-Advance ones, 12 weeks in advance, **(7)**but it's still **worth** trying to buy them the night before.

第18题

1. right 2. symmetry 3. alien 4. harsh 5. seeking

这道题虽然语速并不算快，但内容很多。学生需要集中注意力抓住信号词，具体到这道题就是空格前面的单词。同时symmetry和alien是9分词汇，很多考生可能不会拼（不必太自责）。

Cities are big deal: we pretty much all have to live in them. We should try hard to get them right. So few cities are nice. Very, very few out of many thousands are really beautiful. Embarrassingly, the
使人尴尬的
more appealing ones tend to be old, which is weird because we're mostly much better at making things now: cars, planes, or phones. Why not, then, cities? It's crazy to settle for this and to leave something so important to chance. We need to get more scientific and identify the principles that determine how a city gets to be pretty or ugly.

It's not a mystery why we like some cities so much better than others. This is a manifesto about
宣言
how to make attractive cities. **(1)**There are six fundamental things a city needs to get **right**. One of the things we really love in cities is order. **(2)**Order means balance, **symmetry** and repetition. It means the
混乱的　　　　重复的
same thing happening again and again, and the left side matching the right side. Order is one of the reasons so many people love Paris. But most cities are complete mess. When it's a mess, it seems like no one is in charge. And that's worrying. It's horrible when everything is jumbled up. A pitched roof
乱七八糟
next to a flat roof, a stark geometrical box next to a muddled car park, high rise towers that looks as if they're been placed at random, like teeth in a gaping mouth. We generally have an itch to straighten
渴望　　　把事情搞清楚
things out, and when we can't, it's frustrating. The same urge is there when we look at cities. Often,
令人沮丧的
it's not skyscrapers that we mind in the city, it's skyscrapers that have been dumped without planning,
摩天大楼
like they are increasingly in London, where New York or Chicago shows the ordered way that we love. However, you have to keep something else in mind: excessive order can be just as much of a problem. Too much regularity can be soul-destroying. **(3)**Too much order feels rigid and **alien**. **(4)**It can be bleak,
非常枯燥的
relentless, and **harsh**. **(5)**So the ideal we're **seeking** is variety and order.

第19题

1. lack of   2. associated with; expectancy   3. state   4. interpret; threat

(1) We spend about ten hours a day on average sitting. You know whether it'd be at our computer at work, at home watching television. It's an unprecedented **lack of** activity and **(2)**there's **significant health risks associated with** sitting. Well for instance, decreased life **expectancy**. People do not live as long when they sit more. **(3)**Diabetes risk is increased, obesity, heart disease, cancer, things that you wouldn't intuitively associate with a sedentary **state**. Right and so, when you see people on their lunch

         直觉的   久坐

hour with their tennis shoes on and walking, that's the best thing they could be doing. It is the best thing they could be doing. I would say motion is the lotion. And you know we are designed to move. Ours is a species that evolved with the gill of motion. **(4)**So our bodies **interpret** lack of movement as a **threat**. So metabolically, many things are elicited by that lack of movement, inflammation, diabetes etc,

                                引出   炎症

so it's a significant risk.

        新陈代谢

第20题

1. usernames, passwords 2. tampered 3. voice 4. borders 5. emerges, protected

In today's society, we use passwords to access some of the most critical information for government our businesses. **(1)**We rely on **usernames** and **passwords** to identify people. **(2)**We give them a passport and trust that the picture on it is theirs or the driver's license hasn't been **tampered** with. That's no good enough anymore in the days that we live in. **(3)**Fingerprint, facial, iris and of course, **voice**, that all have biometric patterns to it. For example, the voice has specific points of highs and lows that is unique to you. On your fingerprint there's several minutiae points and Delta patterns and grooves that create a unique ID. So when you come back it can be matched out of many. **(4)**We're identifying people at **borders** with facial recognition software. Even some of the high-end laptops today come with facial recognition software to allow you access to your laptop with a swipe of a finger. You can gain access to your PC gain access for single sign-on to your network. So not only it is secure but it's easy as well. We'll see technology that they're using in Asia with cell phones passing credentials to vending machines for convenience. **(5)**So I think **as the technology emerges,** our **identities will be better protected**.

 第21题

1. sponge; toxins; flame   2. break   3. cross; immunity

What is a microplastic? It's a tiny particle created when the larger plastic items, tooth brushes, bottles, bags break down over decades. They float in the water and get eaten by sea life.

They cause two problems. **(1)**First, the fragments **act like a sponge** to the other **toxic in the water, pesticides and flame** retardants, for example. Suctioning them up and concentrating them.

阻燃剂

(2) Secondly, they are themselves complex polymers, molecules that **body cannot fully break** down.

分子

 (3) When they get really tiny in a billion per metre as a nano-plastic, scientists have shown it can **cross** tissue membranes into fish cells. They say it is harmful to fish, **their reproduction, immunity,**

细胞膜   damage

survival skills. What we don't know what will happen when humans eat fish or sea life. Is it harmful to us? It's already an urgent question. A leading US scientist told CNN plastic is definitely enough in our food and in our drinking water. This is may be something happening to our children. It's already here.

 第22题

1. 2.5   2. over   3. growth rate   4. expected   5. rates   6. level

In 1950, the world's population was **around 2.5** billion. It is more than **doubled over** the next 50 years. In the mid-80s the **growth rate** showed slowed. By 2050, the world's population is **expected** to stabilize, at around nine billion. According to the UN's population division, between 2010 and 2015, around half of the world's people were live in countries with **fertility rates** of no more than 2.1. **The replacement level** of fertility which causes a country's population growth rate to slow down eventually to stabilize.

 **第23题**

1. thoughts 2. source/sources 3. topic 4. punishments 5. expelled

(1) Plagiarism can be defined as the use or close imitation of the language and **thoughts** of another

          refers to   copying

author and the representation of them as ones original work. With the accessibility of materials

through the Internet, students can plagiarise by copying and pasting information from other sources.

This is often easily detected by the teachers for several reasons. First, student's choice of sources are

frequently unoriginal, **(2)**instructors may receive the same passage copied from a popular **source** from

                 teachers

several students. Second, it is often easy to tell whether a student used their own voice. Third, **(3)**

students may choose sources which are inappropriate, off **topic** or contain incorrect information.

                              unrelated

Fourth, lecturers may insists that submitted work is first submitted to an online plagiarism detector. **(4)**

In the academic world, plagiarism by students is a very serious offence that can result in **punishments**

        institutions   impose

such as failing the particular assignment or even the whole course module. For cases of repeated

                   different

plagiarism or for cases in which a student commit severe plagiarism, for instance, submitting a copy

piece of writing as original work, **(5)**a student may be suspended or **expelled**. In many universities,

academic degrees or rewards may be revoked as a penalty for plagiarism.

 第24题

1. determined 2. dictate 3. interpret 4. triggered 5. influencing 6. social 7. tick

(1-2) We are all born with certain physical characteristics **determined** by our genes. But those

aren't DNA **dictate** how we act?. "Genes may very well determine how we behave in given

situations."

(3) Researchers say they are learning now that genes help control how we **interpret** our environment. "There has to be kind of innate circuitry in place that allows us to create culture and

天生的脑回路

acquire culture and do the learning."

(4) But can environment influence which genes are **triggered**? "What really matters is which genes are turned on and which genes are turned off. And different genes are turned on and off in different circumstances".

条件

(5) That leads to debate over the role parents play in **influencing** their children. "Parents aren't the only aspect of the environment. There's also the surrounding culture."

(6) Some believe the stronger **social** influences happen outside the home. "Children live in separate worlds and each world is very important but there's very little carryover from one world to

遗传

the other. And what is carryover is whatever is genetic."

Controversial author Judith Rich says how well a child turns out is up to the child, not the parent. Others find that troubling. "We would encourage parents to be passive or hopeless or helpless in the face of certain challenges that they would assume were genetic."

As the debate rages, what's clear is that as scientists study DNA, they are learning more about

随着争议不断增多

ways to fight disease and **(7)**perhaps understand better, what makes us **tick**. I'm Doctor Dionard dock.

 第25题

1. heavy 2. death toll 3. gone up 4. forecasts 5. 38,000 6. seatbelt/seat belt 7. principal causes

(1) In Europe where road traffic is increasingly **heavy**, road safety affects us all. To remind us of

that, from now on, **(2)**there is going to be a "European Road Safety Day" every year. The aim is the invest as much energy as possible in reducing the **death toll** from road accidents throughout the European union. On the upside, **(3)**the number of lives saved every year since 2001 has **gone up** marketably in line with forecasts. In 2006, twelve thousand lives were saved. On the downside, even if the number of victims is lower, **(4)there is still nearly 38,000** people killed on Europe's roads each year. Some countries have a death toll three times higher than others. So, how realistically can the target of saving twenty five thousand lives a year be achieved? First, continue to address the big three. **(5)**Speed, alcohol or drugs and not wearing a **seat belt**, which remain the **principle cause** of accidents.

 第26题

1. dietary   2. human longevity   3. 1995   4. 115   5. 125 (years)   6. quality

(1) For centuries people have been able to improve their lifespans through **dietary** changes, public health policies and other factors. **(2)**However, a recent study from the Albert Einstein College of Medicine has found that the limits of **human longevity** may have already been reached. In fact, **(3)** researchers believe the maximum lifespan likely peaked decades ago, around **1995**.

According to a news release issued by the school, the team used two different data sets, the 'Human Mortality Database' and the 'International Database on Longevity', as the basis for the study. Based on their calculations, **(4-5)**they concluded that humans can typically live a maximum of **115** years, but the absolute upper limit is likely **125** years.

And while they acknowledge that medical breakthroughs could increase the average life expectancy, researchers believe the maximum will likely remain unchanged. As such, **(5)**they suggest

recommend

that efforts should focus on improving the health and **quality** of life, instead of trying to live longer.

 第27题

1. bump   2. white   3. red   4. particles   5. interact   6. yellowish

Why is the sky blue? Well, first we need to understand a little bit about how light works. When light travels from the sun it moves up and down like a wave, similar to the waves you see on the ocean. Some waves are close together and others are further apart. (1)The distance between each bump in a wave is called the wavelength. (2)And when all of the different wavelengths travel together,

波长

light appears **white** to our eyes. But if you break up sunlight so that the waves are separated, you will see individual colors. In fact, every color has its own unique wavelength. Bluish colors have a short

有点蓝色

wavelength and move up and down more often than **(3)**a color like **red**, which has a longer

wavelength.

So if light from the sun contains all of these different colors, why does the sky appear blue? Well, it also has to do with the way these waves interact with the atmosphere. If there were nothing between the sun and our eyes, the sun would look like a white circle in a black sky. But the atmosphere gets in the way and changes the way the light behaves. **(4)**While the atmosphere may seem like a large empty space, it is actually made up of a whole bunch of tiny little **particles** like air molecules, water,

一大堆的　　　　　　　　　　　　　　空气分子

 and dust. Light waves are tiny too, so when they finally reach the atmosphere they have a hard time dodging the small particles in the sky. **(5)**The shorter wavelengths of light, like blue and violet, move up

紫罗兰色　　　　　　　　　　　　　　　　　粒子

and down so much they tend to **interact with the particles** more often than other colors.

These colors get bounced around so much they spread out through the atmosphere and fill the sky.

不断反射

Even though purple light is also scattering out across the sky, our eye are more sensitive to blue light,

零星散落

an so the sky appears more of a bluish color. Red, yellow, and green colored lightwaves bounce around too, but not as much, and more of this light passes through. **(6)**When these colors are mixed together, they appear a **yellowish**-white, which is why the sun looks somewhat yellow to our eyes.

So, now, you know that when your look at a blue sky are actually looking at a portion of sunlight that has been broken up and scattered by billions of tiny particles.

第28题

1. cultural　2. conduct　3. observations　4. remains　5. tools　6-7. habits;civilizations / civilisations　8-9. gender;attributes　10. array

Anthropologists and archaeologists are explorers of human culture. Their work is closely connected. Both careers focus on the way people live together. **(1)**Anthropologists study the origin of humans and their physical, social, and **cultural** development. They're concerned with how the past relates to the present. **(2-3)**They also **conduct** research by going to locations to ask questions and to make **observations**. And archaeologists is a kind of Anthropologist. **(4)**Archaeologists study past societies through their material **remains**. **(5)**They recover and examine material evidence such as ruins, **tools** and pottery remaining from past human cultures. **(6-7)**With this evidence they build an understanding of the history, customs and living **habits** of earlier **civilization**. Archaeologists often travel to sites called digs where they search from remnants of societies. Together they create a picture of a society. We often think of anthropology and archaeology in terms of the past, unearthing the secrets of ancient civilization. But these scientists also examine living societies in far away Amazon jungles or in a neighborhood next door. **(8-9)**They might study **gender** differences, physical **attributes**, music or religion. **(10)**Their field is the wide **array** of human social experience. Usually their work is sponsored by a museum, university or a foundation but they might also be independent film makers or authors. Most anthropologists and archaeologists prepare for their careers with a four year college program followed by extensive graduate-level study. For many professional positions, especially with universities, a PhD is required. These are academic fields that combine curiosity and attention to detail with a taste for adventure.

 第29题

1. banking 2. marvel 3. boasts 4. via 5. smartphone 6. recipes

South Korea's LG Electronics is **banking** on its new smart fridge becoming an essential

寄希望于……

component of kitchens around the world.

The smart fridge is a technological **marvel** compared to fridges of the past. It **boasts** a food management system that maintains a list of the food it is storing. It also records the expiry dates of the foods and sends out an alert **via** Wi-Fi when that date has been reached.

The information can be accessed via a **smartphone** by consumers as they shop in grocery stores, allowing them to make informed decisions about food purchases. LG adds that its fridge can also suggest healthy **recipes** based on what it knows is inside.

1. tool 2. narrative 3. direction 4. scripts 5. content 6. neutral 7. destructive 8. violence

Video games are a very interesting, powerful and fairly new area of media to consider. One of the really interesting things from a developmental sense is **(1)**they are arguably the best teaching tool we have, the best technologically-based teaching **tool** we have, in the sense that you are not only being exposed to situations and people and concepts, the way you are with television or movies, but you're an active player in them. **(2-3)**You actively drive the **narrative** and you make decisions and choices and moves that will then change the **direction** of what's going on. What that means of course is that this is essentially a virtual reality, that you are immersed in an environment with a set of conditions. That

虚拟现实   沉浸于

you are asked by the game play to behave in certain ways. If you do it really well you get rewarded. You also get more complicated interesting narratives. If you do it badly you get punished. **(4)**So you are inside what psychologists call behavioral **scripts**. And behavioral scripts are how we learn anything. It's how we learn to say "please" and "thank you". It's how we learn to please our parents and to do well in school but if you're in an environment where for example, you are learning how to play soccer well, it will help you learn soccer strategies. It won't help you learn to kick a ball. It will help you think about how to play the game. If you're in a game where you're approaching the world over a barrel of a weapon, and your job is to kill them before they kill you, you will get better at that. **(5-8)**So it really is **content** driven with video games. The medium itself is **neutral**. We give the valence of good or bad or

                                                                                    期望值   引起破坏的

destructive to it. Unfortunately, the most popular video games even among very young kids are the ones that reward you for doing **violence** against others.

1. skills, qualities 2. background 3. goal, experience 4. values, statement

Today, I'm going to answer the question "Why should I hire you?", exactly the way I do in my book 'The Complete Interview Answer Guide'. Now, this is often the last question you will be asked in an interview. Prepare for it. I mean, **(1)**this is your chance to restate the **skills** you possess that are most relevant to the position, and to summarise your other **qualities** that make you the perfect person for the job.

I want you to outline your answer before you go in, and so that you can answer clearly, concisely and with confidence. Your answer should be short, to the point; **(2)**it should reflect your profession, your **background** as it relates to your current needs and the problems of the position. Review the job description and tell them how you are the right person for the job by matching up your skill set with each bullet point for the job description. In formulating your answer, be sure to address these areas:

Number 1: **(3)**Determine their **goals** for the position. This should come up during your research into the company and the position. If possible talk to others who work for the company. If you're unclear on this point, include it in the questions you ask the interviewer, and be prepared to incorporate it into your answer.

Also, show them that you have the skills needed for the job. Based on the goals you've identified in step 1, determine how your skills and **experience** support these goals, and if necessary, you know, just refer back to your list of skills.

Thirdly, articulate shared values. Again, this should come up in your research. **(4)**Look at the company's mission **statement** and regular business practices. Explain why these are in line with your own **values** and goals.

这道题最难的第4题，因为答案位于信号词之前。

 第32题

1. independent 2. builds 3. acquired 4. fashion 5. substantiating 6. argument 7. single topic

"OK, so question one that we've had submitted is: What is a dissertation and what am I expected to produced and achieve? Victoria, should we start with you?"   "Right. **(1)**Well, it's a piece of **independent** research that you do at the end of your university life or I should say undergraduate university life or postgraduate for that matter. **(2-5)**It's a piece of work that **builds** upon everything you've learnt so far and all the skills you've **acquired** along the way, like the skill of telling the audience what you have learnt, the skill of writing it in a proper academic **fashion**, the skill of putting forward an **argument**, defending it and discussing it, **substantiating** it and concluding it. So it's just that. A piece of work showing off what you've learnt **(6)**that is focused on a **single topic** that you select at some point before this year start writing a dissertation that would help and that you work upon over the last year of your study. "

第33题

1. tracked   2. principles   3. series   4. reminded   5. reward   6. mapped out

(1)I **track the lives of 5,000 people** as they attempted to achieve their new year's resolutions. Now, most of failed but 10% did obtain back aims and ambitions. But What were they doing was so different. **(2)**Well, it all came down to five simple **principles**. **First of all**, **(3)**they broke their goal into a **series** of smaller steps. **Second**, they told their friends and family what they were trying to achieve. So that elicited more of a fear of failure but also a sense of support. **Third**, **(4)**they regularly **reminded** themselves about the benefits obtaining their goal. **Fourth**, **(5)**they gave themselves a small **reward** each time they attained one of their small steps. **(6)**And finally, they **mapped out** their progress even spreadsheet on the fridge door or in a journal so they knew exactly where they were. And those the five key principles to actually achieving your New Year's resolutions.

第34题

1. human brain   2. dietary   3. revolution   4. consumed   5. table manners   6. Atlantic Ocean
7. cookbooks / cook books   8. restaurant

And I'm going to be giving a lecture series in February of 2013 on Mondays and Wednesdays; February 11th, 13th, 18th and 20th on the history of food in Western tradition and those lectures will cover four broad and general topics.

The first lecture will cover food in prehistory and the ancient world and we'll think about the origins of cooked food and **(1-2)**the role that cooked food played in the development of the **human brain** as well as ancient Hebrew **dietary** laws and cooking and eating in ancient Greece and ancient Rome.

The second lecture will consider food in **(3)**the middle ages and what historians like to call the spice **revolution** where the way that spices arriving from the far east **(4)**changed the way Europeans both cooked and **consumed** and bought food.

The third lecture will consider food in the renaissance and in particular **(5)**the rise of etiquette and **table manners** and the way Europeans became very interested in the idea of magnificence and the magnificent table as well as Columbus and the new world and the **(6)**Columbian exchange and the types of foods that crossed the **Atlantic ocean** back and fourth after Columbus's arrival in the Caribbean.

And last the final lecture will consider the rise of cooking in France and what we call Nouveau cuisine and **(7-8)**French **cookbooks** as well as the birth of the **restaurant**.

 第35题

1.over 2.controllable 3.admiration 4.reliable 5.cheap 6.celebrated

Well **(1)**the planes being developed by lots and lots of people **over** the years, **(2)**but the Right Brothers certainly made it work and made it **controllable**. Planes existed before, people have made aeroplanes fly before, **(3)**but I always have a huge **admiration** for the inventor who really makes it work, Henry Ford, I have the same admiration for because **(4)**he made a car **reliable**, **(5)**and made it **cheap** and made it work. So the Right Brothers for me are probably the most, should be the most **celebrated** people in aeroplanes.

 第36题

1. specific, hiring manager 2. personality, level of interest 3. dynamic, urge, dive

Tip number one is to make sure to **(1)**address the cover letter to a **specific** person. Generally the person in charge of the department you're applying to or the **hiring manager** in charge of the interview. If you don't know the correct name, we suggest you contact the company and find out who it will be.

Our second tip is to avoid simply repeating the information in your resume. **(2)**Instead use your cover letter to introduce and highlight your **personality**, curiosity and your **level of interest** in the field your applying to work in.

Our third tip is to **(3)**keep it short simple and **dynamic**. Definetely no more than one page and probably closer to a half a page; three paragraphs should do the trick. Resist the **urge** to ramble on and instead **dive** right into the interesting parts right away.

 第37题

1. overwhelming 2. wages 3. household 4. machines 5. managing 6. overdrawn
7. red, interest

If you are looking for a bank account, either because you want a new one or because you're thinking of switching, **(1)**it can all seem very **overwhelming**. Before you look at what the banks and building societies are offering, it's best to start by thinking about why you need a bank account.
房贷机构

(2) Perhaps you need an account to have your **wages** or benefits paid into. **(3)**And you might want to set up direct debits or standing orders to pay your **household** bills. **(4)**You probably want to be able
自动扣款

to take money out of cash **machines** and pay for things with a debit card. So having decided on the
取款机   借记卡

things you need, now's the time to look at the types of bank accounts that are available and work out which one is best for you. **(5)**Current accounts are good for **managing** your day-to-day money. Your wages
活期账户

or benefits can be paid straight in. You can set up direct debit or standing orders for paying bills. You get a debit card that also lets you take money out of a cash point and you usually get a cheque book
取款机   征信

too. **(6)**Most current accounts allow you to go **overdrawn** so you'll have to pass a credit check when
透支   支票

you apply for one. **(7)**If you do go into the red, it's likely you'll pay fees and **interest**. If there's not
赤字

enough in your account to cover a direct debit or a standing order, you'll probably have to pay extra charges.

Basic bank accounts give you most of the same things as a current account. Your wages or benefits can be paid straight in. You can set up direct debits and standing orders and you'll normally get a debit card that also lets you take money out of cash point. The main difference is they don't let u go overdrawn. So there's no credit check to pass and no overdraft or interest fees to pay but they normally do still have charges for refused direct debits and standing orders.

 第38题

1. uncontrolled   2. CURTAIL (=reduce)   3. budget 4. paycheck/paycheque/pay check/pay cheque 5. handle   6. cash 7. spent 8. eye-opener   9. cutting

How to save money and stop spending?

Well first of all, we really need to get a little real here. You're never really gonna be able to stop spending. **(1-2)**So what I think you mean is stop **uncontrolled** spending or **curtail** it. If you're looking at how to save money, and how to control your spending, what **(3)**you really need to do is make sure if you don't already have one, set up a budget. Now before you panic, this isn't that complicated and you don't need a modern computer with tones of software. **(4)**All you simply need to do is to take a look at how much money you're bringing home from your **paycheck**, and over a period of either thirty days or sixty days, try to write down on a simple piece of paper, everything you spend. You can put them in an envelope. You can put them in a folder or files. You can even simply put your receipts in these little white things called envelopes. **(5)**The whole idea is to get a **handle** on how much money

the aim is to   搞明白   没搞明白

you're bringing in and where is it going?Do you know most people haven't got a clue. They just walk

没搞明白

through the day and spend five dollars here and ten dollars here and they say "I'm not spending much". Try this experiment for thirty days. Carry a notebook. A tiny little notebook. And every time you spend anything, **(6-8)**whether you use your plastic or you pull **cash** out of your pocket, record what you bought, where you bought it, and how much you **spent**. At the end of the month, it's a real

eye opener. Now you can sit down and ask:

大开眼界

"OK, this is how much I'm making, these are what I have to pay, my rent or mortgage, my electric, my water, to most of us our cable, but the things you have to, and then you'll have that other little category where (8)you'll see a **whole lot of cutting** you can do. "

第39题

1. active   2. engage   3. probing   4. summarise/summarize   5. nod; silence   6. objective; bias

7. put across

请注意，最后一个空只能填put across，而不是putting across，因为空格前面是to;

Many people think that listening is something they do to feel in a time when they are not speaking. Actually, this is not only wrong, it actually also devalues the person they are talking to because by not listening to them you are really showing a very little interest in what they are having to say and therefore the relationship will suffer as a result.

(1) Take the word "LISTEN" and just use it as a quick reminder of some of **the key skills of active** listening.

"L" for example stands for "look" . **(2)**Look at the person as they are speaking to you; **engage** them with good eye contact.

追问

"I" stands for "inquire" . **(3)**It is used **good opening probing** questions: what, which, who, why, when, and of cause, the good question will start with "how" to really show interest in a person and what they are saying and ask them to open up and tell you more.

(4) "S" stands for "**summarize**" . In other words, what we are really saying here is frequently **summarize** your understanding of what the other person is saying. Use words like "Let me just summarize what I've understood you've been saying or so what you're saying is'. And use a paraphrase to confirm to the other person you've been trying to hear them and listen to them accurately. "T" means "take notes", either jotting down one or two key words as the other person is saying them or using a pattern or technique to build up a mind map of what the other person is expressing.

(5) "E" means "encourage". In other words: smile, **nod** and use **silence** to encourage them to say more. Even little expressions like "aha" or "mm" or "yes", "go on" are helpful ways to encourage the other person to open up and say more. **(6)**And finally, "N" means "neutralize your feelings": stay **objective**, avoid **bias**. **(7)**The person may not be very good at delivery but think about the content they are **putting across** to you. It may be absolutely valid and have a lot of interesting points.

单调的声音

So try to avoid writing people off because perhaps they have slow or monotonous voice and they are not good in expressing themselves. By affectively listening to people, you are not only value them and built relationships with them but you will also seek greater understanding of what they are having to say. And you will learn valuable points in a process. So it not only for their benefits, it's the most certainly for yours.

 第40题

1. mammals 2. energy 3. remote-controlled 4. sensor 5. duration 6. samples
7. flow / flow rates 8. levels 9. exertion

(1) When studying marine **mammals** in the wild scientists data logging tags that temporarily attach to the animals using suction. The tag allow scientists to directly measure animals movement and behavior. While scientists learn a lot from these instruments, **(2)**they want to understand whether the animals behavior or **energy** consumption might be affected by attached tag.

Researchers from the Woods Hole Oceanographic Institution and Texas A&M University Corpus Christi are working with trainers at dolphin quest in Oahu to study the effects of drag created by data logging devices. To do this, **(3)**the dolphins are trained to follow a **remote-controlled** boat while wearing the non-invasive data logger a **sensor** on the boat tracks the dolphins speed and **duration** of

非创伤

the session. The session ends with the dolphin greeting **(6-8)**its trainer in giving a series of voluntary breath **samples** into custom-made device that measure respiratory **flow rates** oxygen and **carbon dioxide levels** of expired gas.

(9) Researchers are able to **quantify the difference in energy exertion** with and without the dolphin wearing the data logger. These studies will help researchers better interpret data in the field studies with wild dolphins and result in the development of even better data loggers in the future.

🔍 第41题

1. traditional role   2. scrutiny   3. range   4. formats   5. driven   6. meet   7. access   8. devices

Academic libraries are changing faster now than at any time in their history. **(1-2)**The **traditional role of the library as a physical space** housing racks of books and papers is **coming under increasing scrutiny**. The library stands at a crossroads. But which direction will it choose?

紧要关头

"Libraries are at a pivotal moment in our history. We're able to use technology and reach out to people around the world."

"In ten years's time, if we were to go and look at university and college libraries, we wouldn't recognise them. I would say, many of them won't exist in the physical state that they do now."

物理状态

(3-5) In the digital age, there is an ever-increasing amount of information available to us. In a wide **range** of different **formats**. And change will be **driven** by the people that use this information.

"The first place I go for information is Google. I actually don't even think about it. I just do a Google search."

"It's quite rare that I actually do resort to printed information."

"Student and researchers find their information needs are changing. I think they're looking for very current, very contemporary information as well as historic data."

当代的

"The students need their information on the go. They're using their mobile devices and they're using their laptops and they're also need, of course, to use the kind of PCs that we offer in the university."

"I usually start with an Internet search for information. And then I will go to online journals or to books. I still rely on actual books for a lot of information."

While demand for change is coming from users, **(6)**it is technology that is making it possible to meet this demand. As more and more resources are available on the Internet via search engines, **(7)** students and researchers now expect to be able to access information around the clock, from almost

夜以继日的

anywhere in the world, **(8)**and via a grow number of devices from laptops to phones.

 第42题

1. cultural 2. external 3. pursuit 4. reach 5. resilience 6. downs 7. supposed 8. human

(1-2)I don't think we have a great cultural idea of happiness. I think many people imagine happiness comes from something external. If you get a new car, a better job, a bigger house you'll be happy, and I don't think that's great of depend on happiness on external things. **(3)**Whenever I hear the phrase, "the pursuit of happiness," the image that always comes to my mind is of racing dogs chasing a mechanical **(4)**rabbit that's always just out of reach. I think a much better goal of life is to be content. Contentment is

满足

an inner feeling of satisfaction that's really no dependent on external factors so in the book I argue that really the goal of working toward optimal emotional health is to **(5-6)**enhance contentment, comfort, serenity and resilience so that you can roll with the ups and downs of life and not get thrown off too much. I think it is not realistic to try to be happy all the time, **(7-8)**we're supposed to be sad or blue some of the time. You're not supposed to get stuck there, but I think that's part of the human experience.

 第43题

1. natural 2. activity 3. global warming 4. factors 5. greenhouse 6. fossil 7. human beings
8. temperature

The passionate eye now returns to the truth about global warming. For the first time legendary broadcaster sir David Attenborough speaks out about global warming.

"The key question of course is how can **(1-2)**we distinguish between variations due to **natural** causes and those variations of the climate that aren't **induced by human activity**. And the key thing that convinced me at any rate was a graph like this one that we marked out on the floor that had been prepared from climate scientists like professor Peter Cox. Now, explain to us the significance of this graph."

"OK, what we're going to do is to take a walk through time. And the first thing to note as we walk through is that the climate is naturally variable. It's a spiky beast. Occasionally, there's a downward trend associated with a volcano going off, to cause a system down because of the dust it throws up, but generally it just oscillates around. And then we get to a period around about 1910 where **(3)**you can start to see an upward trend, a **warming of the climate**, **global warming** if you like. And the issue is, what caused that? Was that humans, or was that natural? So, what we do to try and work that one out is to take a climate model and to put in the various factors. And what we can see with (4)this green curve here is the climate model that includes just these **natural factors**. So this is when volcanoes go off and the output from the sun. And you can see that the green curve here can reproduce reasonably well this mid-century warming. So up to this point, you can reasonable argue that climate variation can be explained by natural factors. But as we move on, we can see that's no longer true as you get to the latter part of 20th century from about 1970 onwards here. You can see the red curve, the observed temperatures and the green curve really beginning to diverge. And the question again is what caused this recent warming? So we're on the model again and **(5-6)**we include human factors, particularly we include the **greenhouse** affect mostly from **carbon dioxide** that comes from **fossil** fuel burning. And then we get this yellow curve and we can see that as well as reproducing the mid-century warming we get this recent rather rapid warming reproduced. And that tells us two things, one is that the model looks realistic. It looks like the real world. And the second thing the model tells us that this recent warming is due to human beings."

"So, there you have it. There seems little doubt that this recent rise, this steep rise in temperature is due to human activity."

急剧上升的

If you look at the green line of natural variability, **(7-8)**it's clear that without the action of **human beings**, there would have been far less **temperature** change since the 1970's.

 第44题

1. minimum   2. leadership   3. draw; profit; family

I wanted to spend a little bit of time today talking about the importance of work experience as you're considering different management programmes. Now this will vary a lot school by school. **(1)** So some schools actually will have a **minimum** number of years of required work experience, so you should enquire with all the schools that you are interested in, sort of, what their recommendations are. **(2)**At Stanford specifically, we don't necessarily look at a certain number of years of work experience, but what we're really looking for are your **leadership** examples that you're able to draw from in your

applicants

life. And as a result, some people actually come to us a little bit earlier on in their careers. So, most years we might even have, you know, one or two students who come directly after university, **(3)**but they've got incredibly strong leadership examples to **draw** from: maybe it is from being involved in

experience in

student government, or **clubs**, or organisations, or starting a non-**profit** organisation, or having been

student politics

involved in a **family** business growing up. So they're able to draw and refer to those leadership experiences in the classroom.

 第45题

1. research proposal; supervisor   2. advertised   3-4. literature search; website

请注意，第三个空格不能填research，因为它是不可数名词，空格的前面有一个定冠词a。

Isla: My name is Isla and I work in the Faculty of humanities and Social Sciences as postgraduate admissions officer that means I'm dealing PhD applications from the point of submission to point of offers being made. The first step in applying for a PhD is to find a an area of research that you're interested in.

Katie: Basically there are two types of PhD that applicants can apply for. **(1)**With the type they develop their own **research proposal** and then seek out an appropriate **supervisor** who is interested

look for

in their field of study. **(2)**And with the second type, they apply for an existing project which has already been **advertised**. Usually on our department's web pages or the faculty website or sometime through commercial websites.

Elaine: I applied for an existing research project but they were happy to allow me to have input into how I would proceed with carrying out the research.

Iain: I developed my own research proposal. So that started obviously we've come up with the idea itself initially. But then also filling out all the forms answering the questions and things like that. So it is was quite a long time process and but definitely a very rewarding one as well.

Isla: If you decide to develop your own research proposal, you must find an academic that will be able to supervise you and whose research interests match your own. You should also try name contact with the academic, so that you can discuss your **research proposal** with them.

Katie: (3-4) Usually they do this either through a **literature search** - looking at the research literature

visit   do

on their **proposed topic** or by **looking** on the **website** and going to the staff pages and having a look at the research interests and the research output of individual staff members. And then selecting a potential supervisor in that way.

 第46题

1. social 2. elements 3. together 4. culture 5. life 6. hospitable 7. accept

(1) Throughout the European union, immigration has become a hot political economic and **social** issue. For decades, people in the European union have rejected the concept of cultural plurality.

多元文化

The idea that different ethnic linguistic and religious groups may enjoy rights and recognition due to

方言

their minority status. But as the immigrant communities continue to grow, **(2)**many ethnic and religious

少数民族身份

minorities are creating identities that combine elements of both cultures.

少数派宗教

"As a British Muslim, I feel very proud to be British and Muslim. As far as I'm concerned, there's no conflict in that. "

矛盾

"There's no contradiction, there's no need for that, you can find a balance, you can find a way. "

"I could never become British, I'm African. "

顽固的   紧紧抓住

Just like in Britain, in other European union countries, immigrants are also stubbornly clinging onto their identity.

"My whole family has lived in Frankfurt for thirty years. We don't feel like strangers. Here we can keep our Turkish culture and tradition, so for us, nothing has changed in thirty years, we're still Turks."

文化认同

Self-definition of cultural identity is what is important in this process. A process which European union is now being called multiculturalism.

there is no

"**(3-4)**Different cultures coming together enriching society with nobody saying this is a dominant culture and nobody saying that this is what we would dictate on other people. Its enabling people to do their own thing but seeing themselves as part of Britain.

"I think we enhance it in many ways you know. And I think the more cultures you get, the better it is. "

入侵   融合

While in Britain, multiculturalism seems to be making inroads. In France, a model of integration which denies the multicultural concept worked well for earlier waves of mainly European immigrants. But it's not working for those from north and west Africa who claim immigrants in France are being denied their own sense of culture. And therefore their personal history and identity.

"Then you hurt them into a ghetto and denied them decent housing, decent jobs and a proper

民主   得体的

democratic voice, no wonder there's a huge gulf between what we immigrants want and what

politicians want to deliver. "

While in some European union countries, multiculturalism is seen as a menace to society. **(5)**In Germany, multiculturalism is becoming part of everyday life. And the city of Frankfurt has even set up a department for multicultural affairs.

多元文化管理

"German and foreign kids are growing up together. They go to the same schools and live in the same neighborhoods. This is an example of multiculturalism.

"Do you think Germany is very multicultural? "

"Yes. Especially Frankfurt is really multicultural. "

"I've learnt a lot from immigrants. **(7-8)**I've learned new languages, to be more friendly and hospitable, how to interact with other cultures and accept them. This is so different from the German way. "

This is Sandra Spencer reporting from the European union.

 第47题

1. time intensive 2. order; coherent; makes 3. difference 4. act 5. undertake

The best way to teach people critical thinking, is to teach them to write.......   extremely

Because what's happened now, **(1)**it's very hard to teach people to write, cause it's unbelievably time intensive. And like, writing-marking a good essay, that's really easy. "Check A" . You did everything right. Marking a bad essay? Oh my God! **(2)**The words are wrong, the phrases are wrong, the sentences are wrong. They're not ordered right in the paragraphs, the paragraphs aren't coherent,

wrong

and the whole thing makes no sense. So, trying to tell the person what they did wrong it's like: Well, you did everything wrong. Everything about this essay is wrong. Well, that's not helpful either. You have to find a few little things they did half right. And you have to teach them, what they did wrong. It's really expensive. And so what I did with this rubric was trying to address that from the production side, instead of the grading side. But the best thing you can do, is teach people to write. **(3)Because there's no difference** between that and thinking. And one of the things that just blows me away about universities is that none ever tells students why they should write something!Like "Well,you have to do this assignment" Why are you writing? Well, you need the grade. NO! You need to learn to THINK. **(4-5)Because thinking makes you act** effectively in the world. Thinking makes you **win the battles you undertake**, and those could be battles for good things. If you can think, and speak, and write - you are absolutely deadly!

 第48题

1. wealth   2. likely, status   3. made headlines   4. nerve   5. consistent

Last night the question was, "Can more money make you a happier person?" Tonight, **(1)** "Does the amount of **wealth** you have, affect the kind of person you are?" . Here's our economist correspondent Paul Saulman, is at it again, part of he's ongoing reporting on making sense of financial news.

In California you're suppose to stop for a pedestrian at a crosswalk. And in a recent study, some 90% of drivers did except for those driving luxury cars like this BMW. They were almost as likely to run the intersection as wait for the person to cross the street. "**(2)**Drivers of those BMW's, those Porches, those Mercedes, are anywhere from three to four times more **likely** to break the law than drivers of less expensive low **status** cars. "

两极分化带来的不平等

In a country more and more polarized by inequality, UC Berkley's Paul Piff led a series of startling studies showing an apparent link between wealth and well, unseemly behavior.

"Oh by the way, there's candy over there. It's actually for children for another study but you know you're welcome to take a few pieces if u want, thank you." That's the script an experimenter recited to every subject, and the results: "Wealthier participants took two times as much candy from children as did poor participants. "

岌岌可危的

Another experiment tested honesty in reporting dice scores when cash was on the line. People all the way at the top who made one hundred and fifty, two thousand dollars a year were actually cheating four times as much as someone all the way at the bottom who made under fifteen thousand dollars a year, just to win credits for a fifty dollar cash prize.

So experimental evidence show that rich people are more likely to break the law while driving, help themselves to candy meant for children, cheat in a game of chance, also to lie during negotiations and endorse unethical behavior including stealing at work. **(3)**The academic paper that resulted **made headlines** everywhere. Wall Street journal article leading with the question, "Ready with pitchforks?"

登上头条

(4) "It is very clear that this study of social class touched a **nerve**. "

触到了……的痛处

Psychology professor Dacker Keltner is Paul Piff's boss and co-author. "We publish these studies in relatively obscure scientific journals and literally the next day we're getting hundreds of emails from around the world, and a lot quite hostile. " "I" ve gotten a lot of vitriol and hate email calling me out for

怀有敌意的   尖刻的批评

junk science and having a liberal agenda."

Hey but wait, didn't those complain to have a point? That the research was done at a famously, some might same, infamously, liberal university. "Hey they're in Berkely, what other results did you expect them to get?" "I regularly hear the Berkely idiot scientist whose finding was what they expected to find. Let me tell you, we did not expect to find this. Our findings apply to both liberals and conservatives. It doesn't matter who you are, if you're wealthy, you're more likely to show these patterns of results. "

(5) Results **consistent** across 30 studies his run on thousands of people all over the United States. So what is it about wealth that might make people behave differently?

1. screen (I think he actually says "screened") 2. drive 3. create 4. scrutiny 5. responsibility 6. leads 7. excellence

Basically we came up with an idea and we called it the "CORE principle". And first and foremost the "C" of the core principle stood for commitment. **(1-2)**And we screen people for commitment. Have they got an intrinsic drive towards achieving a goal? Are they committed to that? Having established that there is commitment, we would then move on and consider the other core principles which is ownership. We like everybody to have an opinion. They like to be asked about their opinion. They don't like to be shouted out. **(3-4)**Create an environment where people are free to speak; they don't feel frightened or under scrutiny to speak their mind. The next step is if you're gonna give ownership to somebody, **(5)**we have to have an all walks of life responsibility and accountability. And it's important I think that accountability is understood and made absolutely clear to very individual, so they understand what they're accountable for and equally what they're not accountable for. So, **(6-7)**I think if you take those four elements, commitment combined with ownership, on top of that you understand and make very clear the responsibility and accountability role, that then leads to excellence.

1. astronomy 2. natural philosophy 3. alchemy 4. 1687 5. inertia 6. acceleration 7. equal 8. opposite 9. reflecting 10. colour 11. calculus 12. minds

这道题语速非常快，还涉及一些专有名词，在听的时候信号词能够帮助学生快速定位。如果前面几个单词写不出来也没事。

Sir Isaac Newton was an English physicist and mathematician, **(1-3)**well renowned for his expertise in astronomy, natural philosophy, alchemy and theology. Much of classical mechanics or the set of physical laws describing the motion of bodies under force are laid out in **(4)**Newton's mathematical principles of natural philosophy published in 1687.

Newton's three laws of motion are perhaps the most well known of his works and cite the following. **(5)**The first law or the law of **inertia** states that an object at rest will will remain at rest.

惯性

And an object in motion will remain in motion unless acted upon by an unbalanced force. **(6)**The second law states that **acceleration** is produced when an external force acts on a mass. **(7-8)**Newton's third law of motion states that for **every action** there is an **equal** and **opposite** reaction.

(9-10) Newton invented the first **reflecting** telescope and devised the theory of **color**. The theory was based on the observation that a prison breaks down white light into many visible colors.

(11) Newton is attributed with the development of differential and integral **calculus** as well as the generalized binomial theorem. He also developed a method for approximating the roots of a mathematical function. A highly religious man much of Newton's writings consist of biblical and occult studies. **(12)**Sir Isaac Newton is considered by many to have one of the greatest scientific minds in our history. And he is buried in Westminster Abbey.

第51题

1. stamina   2. credentials   3. passion   4. independent   5. supervisor   6. institutions   7. contact
8. proposal

(1) The kind of person who should apply for a PhD is someone who's got curiosity, who's also got **stamina**. It's a three-year project usually and it requires a lot of dedication.

耐力   学历证书   奉献精神

Obviously, **(2)**there needs to be some level of academic **credential**, so you would usually require the equivalent of a first class honours or 2.1 honours.

相等的   need

(3-4) You've got to have a **passion** for study, for **independent** work, and you've got to have motivation.

If you don't have research training, we do have quite a number of research training opportunities available here including research methods Master's, which you might take up prior to doing your PhD.

(5) It's really important you find a potential **supervisor** who has expertise in your area of interest.

(6) Look at some of the key **institutions** in the field that you want to work with, and see within that list who is doing research related to your field.

Look around, **(7-8)**find a good person and then try and make **contact** with them so that they will already be **involved in** the idea of your **proposal** as it develops.

 第52题

1-4. meeting; lecturers; small; range   5-8. mixture; vary; theatre / theater; varies

Student A:

第六学级，英国初中最高学级

The way that you taught at university is quite different from Sixth Form and colleges and things like that because you basically have a few lectures but you also have seminars and lectures are usually your whole course. **Meeting** up and just receiving information from one of the **lecturers** on a particular topic. And seminars are where you meet the **small** groups, and you have to kind of discuss the **range** of ideas that you heard in your lecture and to just go through things in more detail. So you get a better idea of what the course is about.

Student B:

At university, your timetable will consist of a **mixture** of lectures and small group teachings which are also known as seminars. Depending on your course, the number of people in lectures may **vary**. For my course we had about 400 people in a big lecture **theatre**. In a small group seminars, again depending on your department, it **varies** between ten people to about twenty.

这道题非常难，并不是来自真实的雅思考试。特别是第一个女孩子，既有口音语速还快，同学们可以多听几遍。

 第53题

1. rural 2. lure 3. shelter 4. sanitation 5. work 6. transform 7. spaces 8. efficient

9. friendly 10. attract

For the first time in history, **(1)**there are more people living in cities than in rural areas. And the numbers expected to double in the next thirty years. "Urbanization is the defining phenomena of the century. Today, as we speak, half the world's population is urban. "

One of the major challenges is that more than one billion people live in slums or squat as settlements. **(2)**Many entice from rural areas by the lure of a better life. **(3-4)**Improving living

吸引　　　　　　　　　　足够的　　　　　吸引　　　　卫生设施

conditions for the urban poor by providing adequate shelter, clean water and sanitation is the must.

"While the incidents of poverty may be more in rural areas, the concentration of poverty is definitely more alarming in urban areas. "

Rapid urbanization is expected to increase built areas by a third, straining services and available space dramatically. "Its very likely, if our current trends continue that the world will urbanize in a very dysfunctional, inefficient and ultimately counterproductive fashion."

功能失调　　　　　　　　　　　　适得其反

(5) One key to making cities work better the experts say is good planning. "What is really needed is long term planning which allows for the reality that, **(6)**to really transform a city so that it becomes beneficial to all citizens, is something that will take, depending on the size of the city, a decade or more. "

城市管理者

Some urban authorities including half of the Philippines 120 cities, have already taken this to heart and are adopting city development strategies encouraged by the Cities Alliance and the World Bank. "You're looking at cities where **(7-9)**you want green transport, you want green spaces, you want energy efficient cities, you want pedestrian friendly cities, you want cities which have housing for all, and at the same time **(10)**cities which are competitive to be able to attract industries and provide jobs to people and attract people into the cities. "

people to come to live there

The hope is that the meeting in Nanjing will unleash further good practical ideas to keep our cities livable in the future.

 **第54题**

1. traces of 2. crucial to 3. carry signals 4. balanced combination 5. energy resources

这道题有大量的专有名词，但其实并不用太过慌张，只需在做题时紧盯信号词即可。

If you sucked all of the moisture out of your brain and broke it down to its constituent nutritional content, what would it look like? Most of the weight of your dehydrated brain would come from fats,
营养成分　　　脂质　　　　　　　　　　　　脱水　　　　氨基酸
also known as lipids. **(1)**In the remaining brain matter, you would find proteins and amino acids, **traces of** micronutrients, and glucose.

The brain is, of course, more than just the sum of its nutritional parts, but each component does have a distinct impact on functioning, development, mood and energy. So that post-lunch apathy,
　　　深夜失眠　　　　　　　　　　　　午饭后乏力
or late-night alertness you might be feeling, well, that could simply be the effects of food on your brain. Of the fats in your brain, the superstars are omegas 3 and 6. These essential fatty acids, which have been linked to preventing degenerative brain conditions, must come from our diets. **(2)**So eating omega-rich foods, like nuts, seeds, and fatty fish, is **crucial to** the creation and maintenance of cell membranes.
　　细胞膜

And while omegas are good fats for your brain, long-term consumption of other fats, like trans and saturated fats, may compromise brain health. Meanwhile, proteins amino acids, the building
　　饱和脂肪酸
block nutrients of growth and development, manipulate how we feel and behave. **(3)**Amino acids contain the precursors to neurotransmitters, the chemical messengers that **carry signals** between
　　　　先驱　　　神经介质　　　专注力
neurons, affecting things like mood, sleep, attentiveness, and weight. They're one of the reasons we might feel calm after eating a large plate of pasta, or more alert after a protein-rich meal.

The complex combinations of compounds in food can stimulate brain cells to release mood-altering norepinehirine, dopamine, and serotonin. But getting to your brain cells is tricky,

肾上腺素　　　　多巴胺　　　血清素

and amino acids have to compete for limited access. **(4) A diet with a range of foods helps maintain a balanced combination of brain messengers**, and keeps your mood from getting skewed in one direction or the other. Like the other organs in our bodies, our brains also benefit

歪曲的　　　　　　　微量元素　　　抗氧化物

from a steady supply of micronutrients. Antioxidants in fruits and vegetables strengthen the brain to fight off free radicals that destroy brain cells, enabling your brain to work well for a longer period of time. And without powerful micronutrients, like the vitamins B6, B12, and folic acid, our

易受影响的　　　　　　　　　　　　　　叶酸

brains would be susceptible to brain disease and mental decline. Trace amounts of the minerals iron, copper, zinc and sodium are also fundamental to brain health and early cognitive development. In order for the brain to efficiently transform and synthesize these valuable nutrients, it needs fuel, and lots of it.

合成

While the human brain only makes up about 2% of your body weight, **(5)it uses up to 20% of your energy resources.** Most of this energy comes from carbohydrates that our body digests into glucose, or blood sugar.

碳水化合物

 第55题

1. elements 2. pain 3. value 4. venture 5. succinct 6. room 7. investors 8. questions 9. answers 10. drawing

If you've got a great idea, but need the cash to make it go, well then you better start working on elevator pitch.

电梯游说

What is an elevator pitch? It's the term used for the two minute presentation, the exact amount of time it takes to go from the lobby to the investors office on the top floor to capture investor interest. Get it right, and they'll invite you into the boardroom. Get it wrong, and they'll call security.

What makes a good elevator pitch? **(1-2)**A good elevator pitch is made up of two key **elements**. First, you have to lay out the **pain** statement. What problem is it that you are trying to solve. **(3-4)** Second, you must show the **value** proposition. How does your **venture** solve that problem. That may sound easy but it's not. Every great elevator pitch must meet four key tests. **(5)**First, it must be **succinct**. After all, this guy's only gonna give you two minutes. Number two, it must be easy to understand. **(6)**There's no **room** for tech talk in an elevator pitch. Both your grandma and your grandkids have to get it. Number three. It must be greed-inducing, **(7)**after all, **investors**

利益诱导

want to make money and lots of it. Number four, it has to be irrefutable. **(8-10)**If your elevator pitch

不可辩驳的

leaves investors with more **questions** than **answers**, well you better go back to the **drawing** board.

 ## 第56题

1. multi-tasking/multitasking   2. sophisticated   3. driver   4. connectivity   5. hunches   6. hunches
7. engine   8. distracted   9. connect   10. missing

这道题有两个空格是hunches，这个单词有点难，不会写也没关系。它的意思是"预感，直觉"。

When you look at the problem of innovation from this perspective, it sheds a lot of important light on the debate we've been having recently about what the Internet is doing to our brains. Are **(1)** we getting overwhelmed with an always connected **multitasking** lifestyle, **(2)**and is that going to lead to less **sophisticated** thoughts as we move away from the slower or deeper contemplative state of reading for instance. Obviously I'm a big fan of reading but I think its important to remember that **(3-4)** the great **driver** of scientific innovation and technological innovation has been the historic increase in **connectivity** and our ability to reach out and exchange ideas with other people and **(5-7)**to borrow other people's **hunches** and combine them with our **hunches** and turn them into something new. That really has I think been more than anything else the primary **engine** of creativity and innovation over the last six hundred or seven hundred years. **(8)**And so yes its true we're more **distracted** but what has happened that is really **miraculous** and **marvelous** over the last fifteen years is that **(9)**we have so many new ways to **connect** and so many new ways to reach out **(10)**and find other people who have that **missing** piece that will complete the idea we're working on. Or to stumble serendipitously across some amazing new piece information that we can use to build and improve our own ideas. That's the real lesson of where good ideas come from. That chance favors the connected mind.

选择题

 第1题

What is Brian going to do before the course starts?

A attend a class

B write a report（Brain已经做过了）

C read a book（课程开始后会有阅读课）

Brian: Is there anything I should do before the course like reading or anything?

Tutor: We prefer to integrate reading with the course, so we don't give out a reading lesson in advance. But we like people to write a case study describing an organisation they know.

Brian:I've already done that as my friends told me you wanted one. But would it be possible to sit in, on a teaching session to see what it's like. I haven't been a student for a while.

Tutor: Fine, just let me know which date and I'll arrange it with the tutor.

 第2题

1 Which 3D printed product can already be bought?

A computers（原文说的是computer models而不是computers）

B glasses

C mobile phones（完全没有提到）

3D printers turn computer models into real physical things. They do this by building up an object in a great many various thin layers. For many years 3D printing has been used in rapid prototyping and to help produce mould masters. But more recently pioneers such as freedom of creation and make eyewear have begun to use 3d printers to digitally manufacture final products or parts thereof.

2 Which **THREE** materials can be used in 3D printers?

A paper

B metal

C wood

D glass

E concrete

眼镜

This means that its already possible to purchase spectacles, furniture and many other items that have been 3D printed and this trend is set to continue. Today 3D printers can build items in a wide variety of materials including plastics, metals, glass, concrete and chocolate. As the technology develops, this will allow an increasing number of parts and products to be stored digitally online. Items will then be able to be delivered digitally across the internet so reducing physically transportation costs and permitting more local manufacturing. Because it's an additive process, 3D printing will also reduce materials wastage as well as permitting high levels of product customization.

 第3题

1 What **TWO** things will the examiner do before the test?

A Ask for a paper driving licence（纸质驾照并不是每个人都有的）

B Check your paperwork

C Speak to your driving instructor（考官会询问你是否需要driver instructor陪同，但并没有和他们对话）

D Give you the option of bringing your driving instructor with you

E Give you and your instructor some feedback（feedback不是考官给的）

On the day of your test, you'll need to take these with you: your photo driving license (you'll need both parts of this), your theory test pass certificate and you're appointment letter or booking number. If you've got an old star paper license, you'll also need to take a valid passport with you. Remember these, or you won't be able to take your test.

When you get to the test centre, your examiner will check through your paper work in the waiting room. They'll also ask you if you want your driving instructor or accompanying driver to come with

give you the option of

you on your test and be there at the end for the result and feedback.

2 Which **TWO** of the following statements are true of the test?

A An eyesight check is not part of the test（视力检查是要做的）

B You can ask the examiner questions about safety（原文说的是be asked，也就是考官问考生而不是考生问考官）

C You have to drive in a variety of traffic conditions

D The test lasts about 10 minutes（考试持续38~40分钟）

E You will be asked to follow signs or spoken instructions

This is beneficial for your driving development so don't forget to talk to your instructor and make sure that they know that this is what you'd like to happen. Your test will last about 38-40minutes. You'll do an eyesight check, **be asked** some safety questions and then go out on the road. You'll drive on various road and traffic conditions and also be asked to drive independently for approximately ten minutes either by following traffic signs or a series of verbal directions or perhaps a combination of both.

 第4题

1 The original buildings on the site were

A houses

B industrial buildings

C shops

There use to be a lot of factories in this area until the 1960's. Creating the park required the demolition of lots of derelict buildings on the site, so most of the exciting parks based all around

　　　　　拆迁　　　　　　　　　　荒废的

you was originally warehouses and storehouses.

　　　　　　　　　　　　　industrial buildings

2 The local residents wanted to use the site for

A leisure

B apartment blocks

C a sports centre

The idea of building a public park here was first discussed when a property developer proposed a high rise housing development. But the local community wasn't happy. If the land was to be

apartment blocks   local residents leisure

cleaned up, they wanted to use the site for recreation. Residents wanted open space for outdoor activities rather than housing or even an indoor sports complex.

sports centre

 第5题

A/D

Which **TWO** facilities at the leisure club have recently been improved?

（《剑桥雅思真题10》Page12）

A the gym

B the tracks（tracks只是swimming pool的一部分，不是主要的facilities）

C the outdoor pool（没有，因为空间不够）

D the indoor pool

E the sports training for children（给孩子的服务升级了，但设备并没有）

Before we start our tour of the club, I'll just run through some basic information about the facilities we have here, including recent improvements, and explain the types of membership available. Our greatest asset is probably our swimming pool, which at 25 metres isn't Olympic-sized, but now we've expanded it to eight lanes, it's much wider. This means there are rarely more than a couple

tracks

of people at a time in each lane. Unfortunately, there isn't space for an outdoor pool here, but the glass roof on the swimming pool is partly retractable, which means you can enjoy something of the open-air experience on warmer days.   可伸缩的

Our recently refurbished fitness suite has all the latest exercise equipment, including ten new running machines and a wide range of weight-training machines. Each member is given full training in how to operate the equipment, and there is always a trainer on duty to offer help and advice. Although we do have adult-only times after 6 and at certain times at weekends, children are well catered for. Older children continue to benefit from a wide range of tuition: anything from trampolining to yoga.

蹦床课

 第6题

1 How does the first speaker describe multitasking?

A it is a myth

B it is efficient but distracting（这与原文完全相反，less efficient且more distracted）

C it reduces the time that tasks take（原文是takes you twice as long，所以不是节约时间而是要花更多时间）

The fact is, multitasking is a myth. Our brains can't do it. You simply become less efficient and more distracted, your error rate goes up 50 per cent, and it takes you twice as long to do the same task. Listen what **Tim Jenkins** has to say. He's the co-founder of **Point B**, a leading business consulting firm.

2 Which **TWO** statements are true according to the second speaker?

A people who can multitask are more effective（原文认为这是fallacy，一种谬论）

B people should always focus on one thing only（原文说的是times，偶尔，不是always）

C we need permission to get things done（是give permission to check out不是get things done）

D the brain is less productive when we are distracted

E organisations are unproductive if they are constantly on-line

谬论

Well, I think there's a fallacy out there, that folks that can multitask are more effective. There are times when it's just important to focus on one thing. I think we also need to give people permission to check out, to check out of the communications network temporarily to get things done; because when you're always on, when you're always online, you're always distracted, right, and the brain really is telling us that that is a very unproductive mode to be in. So the always online organisation is actually the always unproductive organisation.

constantly on-line

第7题

B/D

How to establish a routine for your toddler:

A This is an easy task for most parents.（原文是no easy task）

B The parent must establish a routine before expecting the child to follow one.

C Busy parents need help with their children.（原文并没有说他们需要help）

D Parents should include the child's sleep times in their schedules.

E Meal times don't need to be included in parents' plans.（这个信息与原文相反）

And the topic today is how to establish a routine for your toddler. **(A)**This is no easy task with the toddler. And part of difficulty is that the parent has to have a routine. **(B)**Only the parent has a various

establish

set routine which the child will l follow that. That's a big challenge for parents today who are so busy. **(D)**But the best you can do is to schedule your routine to include your child, make sure you plan for

sleep times

mealtimes, nap times. If you're home for dinner at night, **(E)**make sure you plan for dinner, meals and

need to be included in parents's plans

bath time. All of those things should be a part of your routine. The more routine your schedule is, the more your child will follow behind that.

 第8题

1 Which website are you advised to use when paying for your ticket?

A the East Coast website

B Thetrainline.com（原文已经明确说了don't actully buy them on...）

C the Ticket Alert website（Ticket Alert不是一个website是一个alert，它不是用来订票的）

2 Which **TWO** statements are true of the East Coast website?

A You pay a £1.50 booking fee.（需要付booking fee的不是East Coast而是**Thetrainline**）

B It can only be used for booking trains from London to Edinburgh.（这个网站卖全国的车票）

C You can use it to buy train tickets for anywhere in the UK.

D You will <u>not be charged for using a credit card</u>.

E You can buy a "<u>Super Advance</u>" ticket the night before your trip.（Super Advance只能提前12周预定）

The first thing any regular train user should do is to book their tickets in advance, preferably exactly 12 weeks in advance. Those ￡300 tickets to Manchester, you can get them for just ￡25 return if you go online. You go to a website called <u>thetrainline.com</u>, you fill in their <u>ticket alert</u> system. And you'll get an email telling you when those tickets are available. Because they often sell out very quickly, so when you get that email, act straight away.

鬼鬼祟祟

But, and I know this sounds a bit sneaky, don't actually buy them on **thetrainline.com**, because you'll have to pay a <u>￡1.50 booking fee</u>, and if you're using your credit card another ￡1.50. Instead, pop over to the <u>East Coast website</u>- you'd think that's only trains down the East coast from London

去一下

up to Edinburgh - it's not; they will sell tickets for any trains <u>anywhere in the</u> UK, and they don't charge a booking fee, and they <u>don't charge for credit card</u>. So that's another two or three quid saved.

If you haven't been able to buy a ticket a long way in advance, it is still worth remembering that up until 6 o'clock on the night before, you can still get Advance tickets. They won't be as cheap as the <u>Super-Advance</u> ones, 12 weeks in advance, but it's still worth trying to buy them the night before.

 第9题

1 Many teachers <u>believe</u> that

A plagiarism is <u>not a big problem</u>（这正好与原文相反）

B <u>too many students</u> are guilty of plagiarism

C many students <u>copy each other's essays</u>（学生们抄袭网络的文章而不是互相抄袭）

"Students copying material from the internet is <u>a serious problem</u>, that's according to a survey which found that almost two thirds of teachers reckon <u>too many sixth formers</u> are <u>plagiarizing</u>

many   认为；believe   高中毕业生

<u>online material for essays</u>. Well, Alison Ryan's with us in the studio. She's from the association of teachers and lecturers which conducted the survey. Now, Alison, just how big a problem is this

online plagiarism?"

2 Plagiarism is a problem because

A a student's true level of ability will not be known

B students have to rewrite their essays（原文并没有提到会重写）

C many students do not get caught（学生经常被抓到而不是不被抓到）

"It's a huge problem, many of our members report that is takes quite a lot of their time, quite a lot of work to track it down, but almost more importantly if you'd like or equally important for students is that, they risk getting no grade if they get caught and most of them do get caught and also if they don't get caught, and the very few that don't, they go on the next stage with people having a very false idea of their ability and it sooner or later will catch them up. "

not be known

3 Teachers can spot plagiarism by

A using free software（查重软件是学院和大学付费使用的，不是老师免费使用的）

B comparing different students' writing styles（老师是比较同一个同学的不同文章而不是将不同学生的文章放在一起比较）

C putting key words into a search engine

"Now you conducted the survey. You're part of the group that conducted the survey. How easy is it to sport when someone has plagiarized something?"

"It's actually easier than you might think because it can often mean quite a difference in style from the kind of work that you're kind of listening throughout the year and teachers do know the students that do quite well and will know their other work. It's also just a matter of if you can just go to Google and put in key words and you'll find the same material that in fact the students have probably found. For worst cases or for, if you like, kind of harder cases to spot, there's also certain software like the Turn it in software which is used by colleges, by universities, but there would be a cost element attached to that.　　　　　　　　　　　　　　　　反义词：free

"OK, Alison Ryan thanks very much for joining us. "

第10题

Which THREE of these statements are true?

A The smart fridge is an essential component of kitchens.（这个选项非常诡异，考了一个小细节，原文是becoming，而题干是is）

B It is technologically advanced in comparison with other fridges.

C It alerts users when foods reach their expiry date.

D It can help consumers when they are out shopping.

E It is **able to** make decisions about food purchases.

（smart fridge是帮助consumers做决定而不是直接做决定）

F It can tell users which foods are healthier.（它会提供健康食谱而不是指出哪种食物更健康）

South Korea's LG electronics is banking on its new smart fridge, becoming an essential component of kitchens around the world. The smart fridge is a technologically advanced / a technological marvel compared to fridges if the past. It boasts a food management system that maintains a list of the food it is storing. It also records the expiry dates of the foods and sends out an alert via Wifi when that date has been reached. The info can be accessed via a Smartphone by consumers as they shop in grocery stores, **allowing them to** make informed decisions about food purchases. LG adds that its fridge can also suggest **healthy recipes** based on what it knows is inside.

第11题

1 Which **THREE** things is the speaker going to talk about?

A how to achieve your goals（原文是set goals而不是achieve goals）

B how to waste time（原文说的是**avoid** waste time）

C how to deal with your boss

D how to deal with your advisor（本来是打算谈这个的，但是作者打算扩大范围）

E how to delegate

F how to cope with stress

So, I'm going to talk specifically talk about how to set goals, how to avoid wasting time, how to deal with a boss. Originally this talk was how to deal with your advisor but I've tried to broaden it so it's not quite so academically focused. And how to delegate to people, some specific skills and tools

委托　　　　　　　　　cope with

that I might recommend to help you get more out of the day. And to deal with the real problems in our life which are like stress and procrastination. I mean, if you can lick that last one you're probably in good shape.　　　　　拖延症

So, the first thing that I wanna say is Americans are very very bad at dealing with time as a commodity. We're really good at dealing with money as a commodity. As a culture we're very

商品；有价值的东西

interested in money and how much somebody earns as a status thing and so on and so forth. But we don't really have time elevated to that. People waste their time and it just always fascinates me.

吸引

And one of the things that I noticed is that very few people equate time and money and they're very very equatable. So, let's talk first about goals, priority and planning. Anytime anything crosses your life, you've gotta ask, this thing I'm thinking about doing, why am I doing it. Almost no one that I know starts off with the core principle of there's this thing on my to do list, why is it there?

 第12题

B/E

A Understand what the course is about.（没有提到）

B Think carefully about what they can contribute to the course.

C Tell a story about an experience that they have had.

D ~~Provide a large quantity of work~~ that shows their ability.

E Show an example of their own film work if possible.

F Explain why they are interested in the course.（没有提到）

Students, **(B)**when they're applying, really need to reflect, pause for a moment and think what it

think carefully

is　what they can contribute to the course that they're bringing to the course, and where they want to go with it. We want to see evidence that they do have some experience of thinking of telling stories visually. We don't need to see a great deal; **(D)**they shouldn't panic about quantity,(排除D) **but** they should reflect on what they have got that can show their talent and their creative ability. **(E)**Ideally,

if possible

we would like to see moving image work, but if an applicant has not had the chance to do that, then

show an example of their own film work

they're welcome to show us drawings, photographs, animations - any work that is thinking about telling stories over time.

 第13题

B/C/D

Choose **THREE** characteristics of effective teachers from the list below.

   A They use the largest number of exercises（原文中说需要the largest number of metaphors和 examples，而不是exercises）
   B They know how to choose examples
   C They pick the right technique at the right moment
   D Being older can be an advantage
   E They are chess players（原文中只是说他们like a chess player）
   F They pay more attention to students（原文中是让学生更加pay attention，而不是teachers对学生更pay attention）

There are several things that we know about really effective teachers. One of them is, the most effective teachers have the largest number of metaphors and the largest number of examples to

How to   比喻

choose from, and the best choosing a right one and a technique at the right moment.
   So really expert teachers have to be an old in this. Yes, Yeah, or learn from people like a little fella.

小伙子

   Really excellent teachers have a vast store of move, you think of **like** a chess player, they can go to and giving situations. So the more move you have, you know, the more error and a quiver, the more likely you are able to get through thoughts of moments.

But again, just moving makes different to students to being pay attention. It's also the way of signal you gonna change up.

 第14题

1. B/E   2. C/E   3. A/B

临时抱佛脚

Do you know the most effective ways to study for a test? Do you have to cram or is it better to have a system. Here to help students and parents of students everywhere, Dr.Cynthia Green, psychologist and author of "**Total Memory Workout**". Thank you so much for joining us. Now, what are some of the reasons that we have so much trouble remember things for tests even after we study?

1 What are the **TWO** main reasons why students have trouble remembering information for tests?
A stress（原文完全没有提到）
B nerves（这是第一个原因）
C lack of time in the test（这是迷惑选项，学生是lack of time for the test而不是in the test）
D lack of planning（选这个选项的同学应该是把prepare听成planning了）
E lack of preparation（通过信号词Secondly可以知道后面是第二个原因）
One of the things that happens is we just simply get nervous. Secondly, we don't often leave ourselves enough time to prepare for tests.

2 Which **TWO** relaxation techniques are **NOT** recommended by the speaker?
这里题目问的是以下哪两个缓解焦虑的方法原文没有提到。所以学生只需找到原文提到的，剩下的就是没有提到的了。
A breathing deeply
B counting backwards
C closing your eyes（原文）
D visualising a relaxing image
E counting slowly

Now, what are some of the things we can do to reduce anxiety during test taking.

Well, one of the things is to just practice some, what I call emergency techniques to reduce our anxiety. Some things like training yourself to take deep breaths, to count backwards from twenty or even to have a visualization where you can you know practice beforehand, imagining something that makes you feel peaceful and calm, so that you can have that image, something that you find relaxing and you can go to that place to help yourself calm down.

So, what are some of the stuffs that people can do if they're in the test situation and they realize they're having one of these meltdowns and anxiety attacks and they're not having that recall, what

彻底被击垮　　　　焦虑症

do you suggest people do in that moment?

If you are faced for example with a multiple choice question and you're not really sure how to answer it, then to really work your way around the question, to figure out what you do remember about the question, to try to eliminate alternatives so that you could help narrow your focus, try to

排除选项

remind yourselves of what the main point is around the question and to organize the information in that way to work your way back to the answer.

3 Which **TWO** habits can parents help their children with?

A eating properly and getting enough sleep

B organising their study schedules

C buying the right study guide（原文要求家长work with study guide，没有提到buying）

D breaking the exam down（原文说的是break that study test guide down而不是exam）

E cramming（原文的最后一段其实就是在说cramming的坏处）

Are there specific things that parents can do to help their children when it comes to getting prepared for tests?

One of the best things I think we can do as parents to help our kids is to teach them good test-taking habits. Learning how to take a test is also learning how to be prepared in terms of getting adequate sleep, eating well, dealing with stress effectively and finally organizing ahead of time. So for example, one of the things I've used with my kids throughout their life is to tell them when they know they have a test, to build into their schedule when you know they know that test is coming up, about fifteen minutes a night, every night, to work in preparing for that test. And to work with a study guide also for that test. So they're breaking that study test guide down and learning a piece of it every night. And then using the last couple of nights before the test to rehearse all the information.

When I think back to college and high school, I remember cramming for those exams, cramming that information. I think I actually thought you know, if it's right up there up at the top, newly in my brain, it will be right there. Talk to us about cramming.

The problem with cramming is that we can overwhelm our brains. That sometimes it's just too much information to really effectively keep track of. What I would suggest if someone really has to cram is they try to distill down that cramming to what they really are going to need to know for that test so they are at least trying to place some limits on what they are trying to retain.

 第15题

1 B 2 A 3 B

I want you to take a look at this baby. What you're drawn to are her eyes and the skin you love to touch. But today I'm going to talk to you about something you can't see. What's going on up in that little brain of hers.

神经科学

The modern tools of neuroscience are demonstrating to us that what's going up there is nothing short of rocket science. And what we're learning is going to shed some light on what the romantic

开天眼   透露一些信息

writers and poets described as the "celestial openness" of the child's mind.

What we see here is a mother in India. And she's speaking Koro, which is a newly discovered language. And she's talking to her baby. What this mother and the 800 people who speak Koro in the world understand is that, to preserve this language, they need to speak it to the babies. And therein lies a critical puzzle. Why is it that you can't preserve a language by speaking to you and I,

这引出了一个关键问题

to the adults? Well, it's got to do with your brain.

1 The speaker states that

A speaking a language is a critical skill（原文说的是period不是skill）

B babies are language learning geniuses

C adults cannot learn a new language（原文说成年人学语言有点过时，但并没有说完全不行）

(A) What we see here is that language has a critical period for learning. The way to read this slide is to look at your age on the horizontal axis. And you'll see on the vertical your skill at acquiring a

水平轴

second language. **(B)**The babies and children are geniuses until they turn seven, and then there's

adults

a systematic decline. **(C)**After puberty, we fall off the map. No scientists dispute this curve, but

系统性衰退   青春期   过时了   质疑

laboratories all over the world are trying to figure out why it works this way. Work in my lab is focused on the first critical period in development, and that is the period in which babies try to master which sounds are used in their language. We think, by studying how the sounds are learned, we'll have a model for the rest of language, and perhaps for critical periods that may exist in childhood for social, emotional and cognitive development.

认知

2 The speaker's tests on babies involve

A training them to respond to a sound change

B training them to recognise the sounds of all languages（原文说到研究者会使用sounds of all languages，但并没有说babies要识别所有的语言）

C training them to respond to a panda bear（panda bear会respond babies，说反了）

tests on

So, **(B)**we've been studying the babies using a technique that we're using all over the world and sounds of all languages. **(A)**The baby sits on a parent's lap, and we train them to turn their head when a sound changes - like from "ah" to "ee". **(C)**If they do so at the appropriate time, the black box lights up and a panda bear pounds a drum. A six-monther adores the task. What we have

3 The speaker describes babies as 'citizens of the world' because

A they understand everything they hear（原文说的是discriminate-分辨，而不是understand-理解）

B they can recognise the difference between the sounds of any language

C their listening skills are as good as adults' listening skills（这个信息与原文相反，原文说的是adults can't do that）

learned? Well, **(B)**babies all over the world are what I like to describe as "citizens of the world". They can discriminate all the sounds of all languages, no matter what country we're testing and
　　recognise the difference　　　　　　　　　　　　　　　　any language
what language we're using, and **(C)**that's remarkable because you and I can't do that.

 第16题

1 C　2 B　3 B

1 A year from now, the unemployment rate will be

A fairly good（原文已经明确否定了这个判断）

B not as high in California（题目并没有特指全国失业率）

C very high for the country as a whole

What will the unemployment rate be a year from now? The economy seems to do a little better, and as I said, things are getting worse more slowly. **(A)**And therefore, one might assume that the unemployment rate a year from now would be, well, fairly good or at least not nearly as bad, but I am going to disappoint you. (C)My prediction is that the unemployment rate a year from now is going to
　　　　　　　　　　　　　　will be　　　　　　　　　　　the country as a whole
be 9 or 10 per cent still going to be very, very high, nationally. **(B)**I'm not talking about California, which has been running even higher, I'm talking about nationally. Why would that be? Well, there are two major reasons even if we as a nation enjoy a fairly moderately robust recovery or even any kind of recovery between now and a year from now.　　　　　　适中的　强健的

2 One problem is that

A employees cannot work for more than 33 hours per week（原文说的是average...about，并没有说一定cannot...more than）

B employers will extend working hours instead of hiring new staff

C there are too many part-time workers（很多part-time workers被列为full-time workers）

The thing you need to keep in mind is number one the workweek, **(A)**the average workweek right now is only about 33 hours, which means that when employers get around to hiring people and it's going to take a long time before employers have the courage and confidence to start hiring again. But let's assume that employers start hiring and some industries and some businesses are already beginning. **(B)**It's going to take a long time before they decide they need to hire. Because they can use their own workers. And just expand the number of hours their own workers are putting in. Three, 33 hour workweek means that you have a lot of room to just keep on paying your own workers for more time.

I should add that **(C)**these are not classified necessarily as part-time workers. Many of these workers are classified as full-time workers. They're just working very much shorter workweek. The second thing to keep in mind.

3 If the economy begins to improve

A more people will be discouraged from looking for work（people是因为discouraged而不去look，而不是因为looking for work而discouraged）

B people will think that there are more job opportunities

C there will be an expansion of the workforce（公司会首先在内部扩充劳动力而不是雇佣外部员工）

悖论　有讽刺意味的

And this is one of the paradoxes and ironies of the way we measure unemployment. (is that) As the economy begins to improve, more and more people who have been out of the workforce too discouraged **to** look for work, decide that they might have a better chance getting a job. And so they're going to start looking.

And the Bureau of Labor Statistics measures unemployment in the household survey by knocking on people's doors and saying "Are you looking for work?". And if you've got more people looking for work and fewer people discouraged to such an extent that they don't look then you have a higher

more people

unemployment rate than you do **(A)**when you have a massive number of people as we do right now who are too discouraged even to look. So, for those two reasons that are a shorter workweek **(C)**that is going to permit a lot of expansion of your own workforce before you have to hire outside. And secondly because of the way in which we measure under the household survey unemployment we are likely to have a fairly high.

And, I'd say again 9 or 10 per cent unemployment rate a year from now.

 第17题

1. B 2. C 3. A

1 What is the probability of right-handed parents having a left-handed child?
A more than 10%.（原文说的超过10%是指左撇子在总人群中的占比）
B about 2%.
C about 17%.（这个比例是指父母一方左撇子，孩子出生是左撇子的比例）

It turns out that more than 10% of people, about 10% are left-handed, if both parents are right-handed, there's about 2% chance that your child is going to be lefty. If one parent is left-handed, it's about 17%.

2 What comparison is made between males and females?
A 50% of left-handed people are male.（50%这个比例是指父母都是左撇子，他们孩子是左撇子的概率为50%）
B Males are less likely to be left-handed.（这是跟原文相反的）
C Males are twice as likely to be left-handed.

And both parents are lefties, there's about 50% chance your child is also going to be left-handed. With guys have been twice as often left-handed as girls.

3 A child's handedness can be determined for certain

A when the child reaches two years of age.

B when the child is six months old. （6个月的时候还无法分辨）

C according to which hand the child reaches with in the first year of life. （没有提到first year）

So, how you tell what your child is going to be. When your baby is about 6 months of age, he or she may srtrive to reach with their right hand, but very quickly will bring out their left hand. And it's not until a baby or a toddler is 2 years of age, they can really determine their hand preference.

 第18题

1. B   2. A   3. C   4. A

1 What subject does Professor Wigen usually teach?

A Geography （原文提到Wigen有geography的background，并没有说她teach geography）

B Japanese history

C Map-making （没有提到）

I'm Karen Wiggin from the history department. **(B)**My normal teaching is on the history of Japan and I also have a background in geography. What does it mean for our imaginations for our perception of the world. And for the way we navigate the world that we are surrounded by maps?

认为它们是理所当然的

The ability of maps is really quite recent and the ways in which we use them and take them for granted are quite recent. And, it's as likely that this has affected our imaginations as it is that the creation of the printed book changed our notions about narrative or that the invention of the web

标准　　　　叙述

has changed our understanding of has become another extension of our brains in a way affected the way we interface with knowledge.

连接

2 What will be covered in this particular class?

A The history and variety of maps

B A focus on the most unusual maps（原文提到了unusual map，但它只是研究内容之一）

C The career of famous map-maker（研究map-maker的career也只是内容之一，不是主要内容）

cover

(A)So the idea of this class is that it to create an opportunity to explore the history of maps. When did they really come into widespread usage? The variety of maps both in their design and in their function, the kind of utility that they've had intended or unintended. What's unusual about maps compared to other kinds of texts they are often created by committees. And also the nature of

| 流通 | 商品 | 委员会 |

their circulation as objects as commodities their career as artifacts in the world from the point of creation through marketing distribution, viewing use and ultimately archiving collecting.

map-maker

3 Who will teach the course?

A The lecturer alone

B The lecturer and artists on the web（原文提到了artists on the web，但没说他们会讲课）

C The lecturer and perhaps some other speakers

It turns out that Stanford has tens of thousands of maps, a interesting range. We will also explore the web and explore the ways in which artists are playing with the idiom of cartography in their work.

perhaps 制图学相关的习语

(C)And maybe even have some guest speakers from around campus who use maps in their own work. And many diverse uses that one wouldn't necessarily associate with maps or geography per se.

本质上

4 What does the final assignment involve?

A Creating a series of questions about a selection of maps

B Working with other students to collect interesting maps（原文中说的是学生需要consultation with me-lecturer）

C Analysing maps that the lecturer has chosen（这与原文相反，maps是学生自己选择的）

final

The culminating assignment for this class is a map exercise for their fellow students where they in consultation with me come up with a topic that they are particularly interested in. And I help point

咨询

them towards sources where they collect maybe more maps related to that particular theme. **(A)**And then pull them together in a pedagogical exercise where they create a series of questions that will lead

a selection of maps   教学方法练习

other people into those maps and help guide them in asking both substantive and analytical questions.

引起   本质上   分析

So that they'll actually direct people not force them but compel them just do the sheer interest of

纯粹的兴趣

the questions to really look closely and see what's in those maps and how they mean as well as what they mean. We cannot help but use cartographic representations as we try to warp our mind around

制图表达   搞明白

the big history of human presence on the globe. What is it about us that we are drawn to this medium

出现

as an expressive possibility as a functional utility what is it about our minds and about this form and about the way we move through space and about this form that allows it to have such an enduring hold on human literate societies.